Your Mortgage Matters

Your Mortgage Matters

Mike Smalling

Designed by Vince Pannullo
Printed in the United States of America by RJ Communications.

ISBN: 978-0-578-15343-8

CONTENTS

INTRODUCTION

THE month before I met Stan, I had hit rock bottom. The funny thing is that I was likely the only one who even recognized it. From the outside, everything looked great. I had a nice place and a nice car. I wore nice clothes and had a great job at an accounting firm that most would have envied. But I had something else that was my little secret. I had racked up enough debt to make a gambler blush. In hindsight I know how I got into the situation, but I had no idea at the time how quickly the lifestyle I was living would lead to such a dire predicament. My debt felt like gigantic weights, tied to my feet, pulling me deeper into a financial abyss.

I was headed down a self-destructive financial road in my mid-twenties until Stan showed me how to use some life-changing concepts to make a complete U-turn from the way I'd been living. Looking back, I could not have imagined the impact that Stan's 80% Solution would have on me. Not only did it change my life from a financial perspective; it changed my career path for the rest of my life. He introduced me to some simple, yet significant concepts I will share with you.

I grew up in Bell Buckle, Tennessee, about an hour or so southeast of Nashville. My dad and I visited Nashville often to get supplies for our farm. I'm not sure whether it was my love for Nashville and the desire for city life, or just my desire to get off the farm, but I knew the minute I graduated from high school, I was out of Bell Buckle. I wasn't really sure what I wanted to do with my life, but I knew that I didn't want to be a farmer. I figured the place to start would be to get a college education, so I decided to attend Belmont University. I liked business and was pretty good with numbers, so my advisor there suggested that I pursue a degree in accounting.

I loved my time at Belmont, but that is really where my trouble began. My parents had not done much college planning from a financial standpoint. I had five siblings, so I understand why there was no emphasis on saving for college. My only option at the time, or so I believed, was to take out student loans to pay my way through school. When I graduated, my car was on its last legs. As soon as I landed my first job, I traded it in and bought a new car. I needed something dependable, and the sales guy convinced me that with the great financing the company was offering for new cars, it made a lot more sense to just buy a brand-new one. So, I borrowed and bought. I was swiping my credit card left and right for clothes, furniture, and fun I could not afford. It was becoming a crippling pattern in my life that was out of control.

I had been attending a Tuesday evening church service that was geared toward a younger crowd. It was very casual with the average age of the attendees probably around twenty-five years old. There were no singing out of hymnals and no dressing in your "Sunday best" like I had grown up with. Most of the attendees were single, too, so I had a great opportunity to meet people of my age, who were dealing with similar life circumstances. But the thing I probably liked the most about Tuesday night church services was that I got to sleep in on Sunday mornings. However, on one particular Tuesday evening, our pastor was teaching his lesson out of Leviticus and talking about borrowing money. In one of his points, he stated that "the debtor will always be a slave to the lender." I really don't remember much of the rest of his message that night, but I could not get that thought out of my head – *the debtor is the slave to the lender*. That was how I felt, like a slave. The debt that I had gotten myself into had me in chains.

When I got home that night, I called the only friend I knew who wasn't in a financial situation similar to mine. Frank Johnson had gotten a finance degree at Belmont, so we had several classes together. We both loved basketball, and our friendship gained roots as we became diehard Belmont Bruins basketball fans. Frank was still in an entry-level position assisting a financial planner at one of the most prestigious firms in town. I had never even considered speaking to a finan-cial planner personally. In my condition, I certainly saw no need for any added expenses that life insurance would bring. I was barely scraping by paycheck to paycheck, so there was no need for any investment advice either. However, as embarrassed as I was to call him, I knew that Frank was in a different place than I was. So I called to ask him for help.

We had coffee the next morning, and I told him how miserable I was. When I asked Frank to explain to me how he had avoided getting up to his eyeballs in debt like the rest of our college buddies seemed to do, he got a gleam in his eye and told me about a life-changing experience many years ago when a guy named Stan spoke to his high school senior class about how to manage money.

"Ironically," he said with excitement when he told me this, "the same guy is coming to our office next week to speak to our planners at a dinner meeting! His name is Stan Smith, and apparently he is good friends with our owner and CEO. I saw the announcement come through on a company email, and I recognized his name. I know he won't remember me, but he taught me a couple of lessons that had a major impact on how I have handled my personal finances over the years. I'm pretty sure I can get you in to hear him speak if you are interested. Would you like to hear him?" At this point, I felt like I was a passenger on the *Titanic*, about to drown in what was supposed to be an unsinkable ship. I told Frank that I didn't care what night it was, I'd make it work in my schedule and I'd be there.

My first encounter with Stan put in motion a month-long journey that would change not only my financial behavior but also my life. After our introduction at the dinner meeting and a visit at his office, he let me tag along with him as he met with various clients over the next couple of weeks. I became a believer in his message from the beginning. He hired me a few months later, and I worked with him until the day he retired. The stories and principles I share with you from that first month with him have the power to lead you to a better place financially, just like they did for me. He taught me basic financial principles that anyone can follow, and he showed me how buying a home fits into an overall strategy. I've been helping people learn those same concepts ever since. Let me take you back to the beginning of my journey.

1

THE 80% SOLUTION

ISAAC McClure was probably the most prominent financial advisor around, and his firm, McClure and Associates, was one of the most highly respected firms in town. The firm had devoted more than thirty years to helping some of the most successful people in our community build wealth. Early on, the focus was life insurance sales, but then the focus shifted more to growing clients' investments, while still helping them with insurance needs. This probably had as much to do with the development of clients as it did the firm making a strategic decision to evolve in this manner.

After fifteen to twenty minutes of networking, with Frank introducing me to several of the other planners, we sat down for dinner. Before I had swallowed my first bite of salad, Mr. McClure stood up to introduce Stan. Apparently, this was standard operating procedure for these dinner meetings at McClure and Associates. In an effort to keep the meetings from going too deep into the night and interrupting his employees' family time, Isaac McClure made it a prerequisite for any speaker to agree to make his or her presentation during dinner. I wasn't aware of this ahead of time, but I was thrilled to be jumping right into the true meat and potatoes of why I had come. I wanted to hear from the guy that Frank told me about and see if his suggestions might help me.

"Most of you already know my good friend Stan Smith," Isaac began. "He has been to our meetings several times over the years, and we've talked about various topics related to how our clients' mortgages affect their overall financial picture. I've known Stan since he was a sophomore in college, not too long after we got started here at McClure and Associates, and I don't know if there is anyone on the planet that I trust more when it comes to looking out for the best interests of my clients, particularly in mortgage financing.

"I'm guessing that for those of you who know Stan personally, you have already recognized the unique approach he gives his clients from a coaching perspective – something that is not really that common with most mortgage loan officers. Tonight, as opposed to asking Stan to dig deep into a specific topic like he normally does with us, I've asked him to share more of his big picture version of how he counsels people. He has graciously agreed to do that, so without further delay, please welcome my buddy, Stan the Mortgage Man!"

As Stan walked up to the makeshift stage that had been set up in McClure's main conference room, the background music started playing "Rocky Top," and it got louder as he approached the microphone. I didn't get it, but obviously most of the folks in the room did as they busted out in laughter first and then started cheering and clapping along to the song. When Stan got to the stage, he was pumping his fist in the air, encouraging those who were clapping, and he exclaimed, "Very nice! There is nothing like the greatest college fight song to get the blood pumping." He actually got a little bit of a mixed response from that comment. Being a guest, I sat quietly. But had I known him better at that point, I might have let out a "Boo!" After all, this was Nashville, not Knoxville. We had our own team, and it wore black and gold, not that gaudy orange. But it was obvious that this was all in fun. I'd seen Isaac's biography and knew that he went to the University of Florida. So I'm sure he and Stan had some fun with that as well.

Based on Isaac's comments about how long he'd been working with Stan, I guessed that Stan was probably in his mid to late fifties, but he seemed much younger to me. "Thank you so much for the opportunity you have given me to visit with you tonight," Stan began. "I know how important your time is, but I also know how dedicated each of you is to helping your clients succeed with the financial aspect of their lives. Knowing that, it doesn't surprise me to see this room full tonight. It is a reflection of your dedication, and I'm honored to be in your presence. While I think a person's mortgage is close to the top in financial importance, it is still just one piece of a much larger financial puzzle. You guys handle just about every other piece of that puzzle, so your role in your clients' lives is much more critical than mine. But when we work together, we have the opportunity to create a strategic plan for our customers that has great potential for their success and minimal flaws if they follow the plan."

He continued, "For many years, I've been teaching clients a concept I nicknamed the 80% Solution, and Isaac has asked me to share the basics of the plan with you. But before we get into that, I want to tell you a little bit about why I think the plan is so critical. In reality, the idea is nothing earth shattering, and it is probably something you have been advising for years in some form or fashion. I simply want to tell you some of the logic behind it before going into the nuts and bolts so that you will better understand why it is so important to me. I'd also like to ask you to write down any questions you have as we go through the material. We will spend time at the end of my talk going over the questions that you have.

"You see, I've found that the main reason people struggle with their finances is one of two things: they overspend, or they don't have enough money socked away that is available when life throws the proverbial curveball. Many times the two go hand in hand. And frankly, I'm not sure why people call them curveballs. It would be great if all we ever saw were fastballs and could just sit back and wait for one to come down the middle of the plate before taking a swing. But life is just not like that. For 99% of us, we should recognize that at some point in time, the unexpected is going to occur, and there will be a need for cash that isn't available. So to cure that, we have to figure a way to get our clients to spend their money in more of a limited manner that is reflective of their earnings, and we have to help them save in a deliberate manner. It's tough to do that because most of our clients have grown up in a world where only the here and now matter. Unfortunately our government teaches us that it is okay to spend more than we make, and we can just pay for it later."

He paused for a moment as he and I made direct eye contact. I know it was just a coincidence, but I felt like he was talking directly to me.

He continued, "I know the goal of each of you in this room is to help grow your clients' investment base. This not only helps them; it helps you as well. So it is important to understand a little of the philosophy behind the 80% Solution so you can see how it helps your clients accomplish this.

"Too often, people view money as nothing more than what is needed to get them from one month to the next. It becomes a revolving door of money in so that it can go right back out to meet the demands of life. It's a cycle that most can't seem to stop without a plan of action. We need to be teaching them that money is not static. It is alive and always at work. The key is to make the money work for us instead of the other way around. To do that, there must be boundaries, and there has to be a predetermined framework with which to make that happen. Knowing that, I coach my clients to follow the 80% Solution. And even though 80% is a specific number and has significance, the reality is that it is as much a concept, or really a process, as it is a target.

"The 80% Solution has two parts. First, an individual simply has to have a monthly budget where all expenses are covered by 80% of his net income, allowing him to give and save the first 20%. Second, he ultimately owns a home with no more than 80% of the home's value tied up in a loan, and that is his only debt. That's it. I told you it wasn't rocket science. I just wish it was as easy to live out as it is to state."

This hit me like a ton of bricks. Was he kidding about 80%? My expenses were at 100% of my net income, and most months I struggled to keep it at that. How in the world was I going to get my expenses down to 80% of what I was bringing home?

"There is something else I'd like to make clear about this," he said. "My suggestion is that someone give away 10% of the extra 20% and save the other 10%. I realize that only saving 10% of net income will not necessarily solve all of the long-term financial needs that your clients will have. And this is particularly the case if the savings part doesn't get started until later in life. The later someone starts saving, the larger the percentage he will need to save, especially for retirement. So someone not starting this plan until his thirties or forties may have to figure a budget that requires him to live on less than 80% so there is more available to save."

He paused and then said, "The issue that I come across most often is that folks are barely saving anything if at all. And more important, they don't have a plan. I believe that if someone starts out from the very beginning of his adult life following the 80% Solution, he will save what is necessary, and he will develop a lifestyle that is focused on saving and giving that will ultimately lead to saving a lot more than just 10% of net income. But there has to be a minimum standard, and I believe that giving 10%, saving 10%, and living on 80% should be it.

"I want to share with you some financial stages, or levels, that I believe all of us go through at some point in our lives," Stan continued. "And while my goal is to ultimately get clients to Stage 5, in which they have accomplished the 80% Solution, Stage 6 is where they become really profitable clients for you. At Stage 5, the client has living expenses less than or equal to 80% of his net income, he has an adequate emergency fund, he has no debt other than a mortgage, and his mortgage is paid down to 80% or less. Beyond that stage, what we'll call Stage 6, is where the client will fit nicely into your care. This is when the primary focus becomes all about giving and investing. While someone may have some components of each of these stages at all times, to get to each progressive stage, certain criteria have to be met or removed to go to the next level. I believe that you will easily recognize that each of your clients fits into at least one of the progression of stages.

"How many of you have seen Disney's *Meet the Robinsons?*"

He looked around the room, and about half of the hands went up.

"Let me tell you that it is very possible for someone to regress and move backward, even after reaching a higher stage. We never want to see that happen, but it is not unthinkable. In those cases, we encourage them to begin the progression again, and like Cornelius Robinson, we . . ." He paused to see if anyone would finish the statement.

Well, here is where having so many younger siblings paid big dividends for me. I was a Disney whiz and easily knew the next line. So I yelled out, "Keep moving forward!"

Stan quickly looked at me and said, "That's right, young man. Failures will come. It's okay. Embrace them and keep moving forward. For most people, the progression to financial success is made over a long time period; for many, it is a lifetime. My hope, and I believe yours as well, is to shorten the time period of each stage for our clients. Remembering that this is a process, let's take a few minutes and review each of the stages.

"To help make explaining this a little easier, I've come up with a chart that is similar to the stages in Maslow's Hierarchy of Needs. In a similar fashion, where the bottom level of his triangle is meeting physiological needs, then moving up through safety, love/belonging, esteem, all the way to the top where self-actualization is the driving force of human nature, we start at the bottom, where your clients are riding the month-to-month merry-go-round of just getting by, and move them all the way to the top where they are living out the 80% Solution. By taking them to the pinnacle of the triangle, you've helped them move from a life of just getting by to where they can be a force for good with their finances.

Stage 6:
Investing
Giving

Stage 5:
All non-mortgage
debt paid and
mortgage paid
down to 80%

Stage 4:
Homeowner
More saving and more giving

Stage 3:
Any credit issues are resolved; Paying
down of non-mortgage debt has begun;
Saving (particularly for down payment) has
begun; Gifting has begun

Stage 2:
At 80% budget for expenses compared to net income
Emergency fund (3 months) established

Stage 1:
Not at 80% budget, No emergency fund (EF), Possible credit issues, Non-mortgage debt, Little or no savings, Not giving, Renting

It took me all of about five seconds to see that I was sitting dead in the middle of Stage 1, at the bottom of the pyramid. I didn't have any credit issues because I always paid my bills on time. But I certainly had way too much outstanding credit, had no savings, was renting, and wasn't giving any money away. That sinking feeling started coming over me again as I felt the weights pulling me so deep into the water that I could hardly see light.

But I snapped out of it as Stan continued, "As you can see in Stage 1, none of the desired financial criteria is being met. This is typically someone just getting started out in life. He is spending too much, not saving or giving any money, likely has credit issues (either bad or not enough), is renting, and is just pretty clueless all around from a financial sense." He never looked at me, but I felt as if he was talking directly to me and no one else was in the room.

"But don't be fooled," he added. "It could just as easily be someone much older, who has never gotten serious about getting the financial part of his life in order. The primary components of moving into Stage 2 are for the client to establish a small emergency fund and structure his budget to where he is spending only 80% of his net income on his monthly expenses. For many clients, fixing the budget is by far the most difficult thing to get a handle on. It will likely require a significant amount of desire and discipline because he will be asking himself to live differently."

He looked around the room. "No longer is he allowed to spend every penny on 'fun stuff' and live month to month. He begins to tell his money where to go and not vice versa. Until he understands the importance of living within his means, he can accomplish nothing else. But once he does come to this realization and he makes it a part of his everyday life, anything can be accomplished. And I mean that. If you can get your client to commit to living within 80% of his net income every month, when he is currently not doing that, you will be able to help him get on the road that will ultimately set him free from a lifetime of financial burden."

Stan had nailed me with this simple statement. Like it or not, this is where I was. But more important, and maybe for the first time in a very long time, I had a glimmer of hope and knew that this is where I needed to begin. My situation wasn't as hopeless as I'd made it out to be. Sure it seemed that way to me at times. But I created it. I was also the only one who could fix it. Despite the urge to get up right then and there and immediately put a plan in place for myself to minimize my monthly expenses to 80% of my take-home pay, I decided that it would be a good idea to hear the remainder of what Stan had to say. I needed more help in getting a vision for where I was going. I was already determined to get out of Stage 1. So let's see where I needed to go from there.

Stan was rolling at this point. "Establishing a basic emergency fund is also critical in moving from Stage 1 to Stage 2. Having this type of account prevents the potential debt hole from growing. As I'm sure you would agree that you want this for your clients as well, I love it when my clients maintain a minimum of six months' worth of expenses set aside in a cash reserve account that is fully liquid at all times. That means if your client has monthly expenses of $3,000, she has $18,000 in an account that she is not going to touch. In the beginning, I'd settle for somewhere between one and three months. That should at least give her enough of a cushion to withstand most emergency needs for cash in a month. Having six months is better, and that will be a condition for a future level. Heck, do you know how much freedom you give your clients when you help them establish a twelve-month emergency fund? That means they can go a whole year jobless without missing a beat. That is a very comforting feeling. But we'll call it an even three months to get the emergency fund in place, living on 80% of net income, to move out of Stage 2 and into Stage 3.

"Once your client has moved into stage 3, he must clean up any credit issues and start establishing a solid pattern of saving and giving money, while starting to pay off non-mortgage debt. There are not any specific targets related to debt reduction at this point, just progress. The amount of outstanding debt and the type will determine the amount of progress that needs to be made. However, any existing delinquencies arising from credit issues need to be cleaned up immediately at this stage. If there are existing issues that need to be resolved from a credit standpoint, such as outstanding delinquent accounts, there also needs to be sufficient time to allow the credit score to improve so that credit will not be a deterrent to purchasing a home, which will come in Stage 4. But it will be important to have a good target of the amount of money to be saved for a home purchase. This will serve as the target for short-term savings.

"Also, this is a good time to establish credit if there isn't any. If my clients have no credit at this point, I normally suggest that they open a couple of no fee credit cards with minimal availability. No fee simply means that there is no annual fee, and minimal availability typically means having a line available of up to $500.

"My suggestion to clients is to use the card or cards to pay standard monthly expenses that they would have anyway. Things like gas and groceries are ideal. Because it is a little easier to turn over a piece of plastic versus actual cash, it is preferable if the cards are used in this manner. That way they are not paying too much or buying things they don't really need. The reality is that if the cards are used in this manner—not overspending and paying the balance off each month— they get to take advantage of keeping the cash in a checking or savings account the extra period between when the purchase was made and when the bill comes due. Every penny adds up.

"After twelve months of having the accounts opened, the credit score should be established in good order with a decent enough score to obtain mortgage financing. And it is probably a good idea to suggest that they not use the cards and keep a zero balance on them for at least two months prior to applying for a mortgage loan so that when their credit is pulled, the balances are zero. It will help the score to have these open accounts with full availability, particularly if the available limits are small. I suggest a small availability for clients new to credit cards. This will prevent them from getting into any trouble by spending too much. But when the availability is small, say $500, it is very easy to get a balance over 50% of availability. And when revolving debt has a balance that is higher than 50% of availability, it can cause the overall credit score to drop. So coach them on that. It is important to pay off any delinquent items, and it is good to have established credit as well."

Stan stopped to take a drink of water before continuing, "Once your clients have moved into Stage 3, they will have reduced expenses to 80% of net income so there will be 20% left over to use toward the other goals of saving, giving, and starting to pay down non-mortgage debt if there is any. This, too, is a process and must be taught to most clients, particularly if they have been in the monthly merry-go-round of spending everything they make. But this will give them the ability to pay down debt and save money. I believe that it is also a critical component of our jobs to teach our clients to be generous with their excess and equally important to teach them to be diligent with their savings efforts. Both exercises need to be in place before they can leave Stage 3.

"If you have a client who is not accustomed to giving any money as part of a monthly habit, I suggest you help him start slow. You have helped him establish a budget that will allow him an extra 20% of net income to go toward discretionary items. These items need to be saving and giving related. While my personal belief is that it should be split 50-50, to where 10% is saved and 10%

is given, I would not expect someone who has never been accustomed to giving money away to be ready to make that kind of commitment required to give a full 10% of his monthly net income at this stage. I suggest that the client designate at least $100 a month for something specific that is charitable – preferably something that he is interested in helping. Doing this will also allow him to put more money into savings and give him the opportunity to be excited about watching those savings grow. At this stage, you are helping him create momentum. And remember that momentum comes from energy, and energy comes from progress. So as your client sees progress being made, he will be energized to do even more.

"Because the significant step in Stage 4 is purchasing a home, during Stage 3 your client will need to be taking steps toward that. His situation will determine whether it's more important to allocate more funds toward savings or toward paying off non-mortgage debt. I like the idea of saving first because your client can always take money that's been saved and use it to pay off debt later. There has to be a balance here, though. You don't necessarily want your client saving in an account that pays very little interest while paying double-digit interest on credit cards. You may need to provide some coaching at this point.

"A mortgage loan requires specific debt ratios or limits how much can be spent on debt versus income on a percentage basis. So the client might need to focus a little more on paying down debt versus saving. In that case it is somewhat of a two-step process and may take a bit longer. That is why you want to help him build momentum. Momentum will help carry him through the longer period of accomplishing what he is setting out to accomplish. Stage 3, just like the entire process of the 80% Solution, is also a work in progress. But to exit Stage 3, your client has to have clean credit and be working toward more saving, more giving, and paying down non-mortgage debt.

"In Stage 4, your client becomes a homeowner. Along with establishing an emergency fund equivalent to six months' worth of expenses, this is the primary goal in Stage 4. It's great if your client can establish the six-month emergency fund before owning a home. But understanding that much of the effort toward saving may have been going toward establishing a down payment, it might not be realistic to also expect him to be able to save an additional three months toward an emergency fund during that process.

"Increasing the emergency fund is important because there is now a mortgage to pay, and having a bigger cushion is a safer place to be. The same rule applies here, though, about saving at a rate earning virtually no interest, while paying out debt at a significantly higher rate; paying the debt down is likely the better choice.

"Once the home is purchased, and the emergency fund has been fully established, you should encourage your client to focus full attention on paying off all non-mortgage debt. It's likely that there is no tax benefit to paying those debts, and the rates are probably above what you could realistically invest the extra money on his behalf. I'm not suggesting that continuing to save is unimportant. We all know that the sooner money is invested, the longer it has to grow, so this is still a key component. It's likely that your client's life may have even changed during these first few stages. He could now be married; he may have children; he may even have a new job. Saving for college and retirement plays a role during this stage as well. I also believe at this stage, you can encourage your client to start giving more. It is amazing the natural process that takes place when someone starts to gain control of his financial destiny. His heart just seems to grow in the process, and he will begin looking for more opportunities to be generous.

"Stage 5 is all about debt removal. By the time your client leaves Stage 5, he will have his mortgage paid down to 80% of the value of the home, and he will have no debt other than the mortgage. My recommendation almost 90% of the time is for a client to pay all other debt completely off before going to work on paying down the mortgage. There might be an exception, such as a student loan with an ultralow rate, where the loan might not need to be paid off before attacking the mortgage debt. But those situations are few and far between. Typically the mortgage rate will be lower than other debt, and it has the tax benefit of paying the interest. So it makes sense to pay the other stuff first.

"From a strategic standpoint, your client is still saving, giving, and paying down debt during Stage 5, just as he was in Stages 3 and 4. There is just a strategic target of paying off everything but the mortgage and paying the mortgage down to 80%. When the client has moved on from Stage 5, he will have reached the 80% Solution–living on 80% or less of net income with no debt other than a mortgage that is paid down to 80% of the home's value.

"At this stage, your client has plenty of discretionary income available for saving and giving, so you are an incredible resource for him. If he has paid off debt and kept the same lifestyle from an expense standpoint, more than 20% of his net income will be available for giving and investing. He is going to depend on you to help him grow the various investment accounts that will help pay for needs and wants down the road. This also makes him a key asset for you; he should be very a profitable client. Your role now is to help your client not only build wealth for the future but also create a situation where he can work toward a goal of living on passive income. If you can give your client both the vision and the strategy of creating a scenario for himself that he is earning enough passive income to one day support his expenses, you will have set him financially free, and you will have earned a client who is a raving fan. He will sing your praises and be a huge referral partner. It is a win-win for everyone!"

That completed Stan's presentation, and he answered questions for another half hour before Isaac stood up and called the discussion to an end. I had been taking notes so feverishly that I did not even realize how late it was. After Isaac thanked Stan and gave him a mocking Gator Chomp, waving both arms up and down together in a motion mimicking an alligator, he dismissed the group. I made a beeline straight to Stan.

Several beat me to him, but I was happy to wait my turn. When I finally got to meet him, I asked, "Can I come to your office one day and visit with you?" I'm not sure whether he sensed my desperation or whether he had been so impressed by my Disney knowledge that he felt compelled to oblige.

He saw my nametag, which was a giveaway that I was not an employee of McClure and Associates, and said, "Sure, Mike, how about Monday morning at 8:00?"

I was floored. "I'll be there," I responded.

As I turned to walk away, he said, "Hey, keep moving forward!"

What I learned from the meeting with the financial planners:

1. *There is a big picture when it comes to my finances, and it can be broken down into stages (I was clearly in Stage 1).*
2. *People fail financially because they overextend and don't have adequate savings.*
3. *Everything related to personal finance is a work in process.*
4. *At a bare minimum, I need to be giving 10% of my net income away, saving 10%, and living on the remaining 80%.*
5. *The most important thing is progress — keep moving forward.*

2

MY FIRST MEETING WITH STAN

STAN'S office was actually a house that had been converted into commercial property. I was familiar with the area since it was only about half a mile from Belmont's campus. It was just outside downtown Nashville and one street over from Music Row. That was pretty fitting as I would learn very soon because Stan was quite the country music fan. The sign out front displayed the My Home Mortgage name seen from the street, and the logo accompanied the name on the wall behind the reception desk.

When I walked in, a young lady, who could have easily been mistaken as a country music star, came out decked in jeans and very nice cowboy boots. She greeted me with a Southern, "Hi, you must be Mike," and put her hand out to shake mine.

I wanted to say, "Howdy," but I restrained myself. I said, "Yes, ma'am, I'm Mike."

She asked me if I'd like anything to drink and invited me to have a seat. She said Stan would be with me in a moment.

Within two minutes, Stan was standing before me, reaching his hand out to help me up from my chair. Even though Stan was a big guy, my guess is that he was at least 6'6", he was very soft spoken and somewhat of a gentle giant. All I really knew about Stan thus far was that he had some pretty interesting thoughts on how finances should be handled and that he was a Tennessee Vols fan. If I hadn't known the second of those two points, I would have immediately become aware of that fact as we walked into his office. Sitting right there on his desk was an authentic Tennessee football helmet with someone's signature on it.

He saw me staring at it and said, "Coach Fulmer and I played together at Tennessee, so I got him to sign that for me when he started coaching up there."

As I glanced around the room, I saw pictures of his family and more pictures than I could count of him with various country music singers. I'm not much of a country music fan, but I recognized Garth Brooks, George Strait, and Alan Jackson. I asked him, "Do you like country music, or have you actually worked with all of these folks?"

He said, "A lot of one and a little of the other. Being here in Nashville gives me the chance to occasionally help out a young up-and-comer. Most of the time, once somebody hits it big, he or she doesn't have a need for my services anymore. And good for them! But yes, I am a pretty big fan of all of 'em."

With that, we sat down, and he continued, "Mike, I really have no idea why you're here. Well, I have my guesses, but I'll let you tell me about that. I certainly sensed in our brief encounter that this was important to you, so here we are."

For the next twenty minutes I explained to him my predicament and how I got into it. I told him about my family, growing up in the country, my education, my current job, and yes, I told him all about my current financial crisis. For the second time in less than two weeks I was coming clean about my little secret. He nodded several times and never lost eye contact with me. He was very in tune with what I was telling him, and I could sense his compassion. But I could also tell that this was not the first time he had heard a story like mine.

When I finished, he said, "Mike, I want you to take just a minute and think about the significant things in life that people take time to plan out." I had no idea where he was going as he paused for a moment to let me think but then continued before I could respond.

"Some people will take six months to plan that great vacation detailing every minute of the trip to make sure that the time is maximized. Most wedding engagements last up to a year, and everything from the type of flowers chosen to where grandma is going to stay fills up the minute details. As you are probably aware from recent experience, high school juniors and seniors spend an enormous amount of time looking at colleges and deciding what to do after graduation. Others may take months to buy a car, scouring *Consumer Reports* to find the best options and then even more time driving from lot to lot, seeking out the best deal once a vehicle option has been chosen. What about having a child? Not only are there nine months of pregnancy to get prepared for the new child, but for most, much thought and planning go into the decision before getting pregnant in the first place.

"These are all incredibly important events. Some are life changing and deserve our time and attention to detail when planning them. During the planning of these and other significant events of life, how much of the planning time do we spend figuring out our method of paying for the event? For that matter, how much time do we really spend planning our finances and how we will pay for most of the things we purchase – little things like buying lunch or the big-ticket items like a car and a home?"

I wasn't really sure but was about to respond when he continued, "And while buying a home certainly should require the same sort of planning and thought process, it amazes me how so many people fail to plan out the financing of a home purchase. A lot of detail goes into figuring out the *where* and *what* of buying a home. What is the best part of town to live in? Will this be a good home for my family? What are the schools like? How much space do we need? Do we want a big yard? But it is the *how* that is forgotten. Other than trying to figure out whether or not they qualify for a loan, not much other consideration goes into how the loan is going to get paid back and how it fits into the borrower's overall budget. Those things rarely get the consideration necessary for such a significant investment. Why is that?" He paused and waited for my answer.

"I'm not really sure," I answered. "I guess people just get so busy living their lives that they do what they see everyone else doing at whatever phase of life they are in. I assume that is what most people do. They buy the home that is appropriate for whatever stage of life they are in."

"I get that," he replied. "But I'm also wondering if that is what has you in this predicament with your finances. It appears that you've just done what everyone else has done and bought what everyone else has bought without much consideration to how you are going to pay for it, other than assuming you'll pay for it later. I know that most of the stuff I just mentioned, probably other than buying a car, you haven't done yet. But you've clearly made intentional purchases without considering the consequences of the payments. What prevents us from considering the financial implications that exist when we buy stuff? Why do we buy things we can't pay for on the spot, particularly if we don't need that particular thing at the time to survive?"

"I think in my case," I replied, "a lot of my purchases have been because I felt like I really needed those things when I got them. Like my car, I needed that to get back and forth to work. The clothes I had coming out of college definitely weren't going to work in the business world, so I upgraded my wardrobe. I needed to furnish my new apartment, so I did that too. I guess my thought process was that those would all be one-time expenses that I would have plenty of time to pay for later. I really didn't count on the fact that the payments would consume everything I was making."

Stan nodded and then changed directions a bit. He said, "For most Americans, buying a home is the largest financial investment that they will ever make. I'm not discounting any of the events I mentioned before or the ones you've referenced, but none of these have the typical impact from an overall financial standpoint as buying, and ultimately financing, a home. I mention that because helping people buy homes is what I do for a living, and I see your situation daily with people who are trying to buy a home. It is no different with that purchase than it is with any other. There needs to be a plan in place when borrowing money as to how it fits into an individual's overall financial picture and what the best route is to pay off the debt. Knowing that, it shocks me how haphazardly the normal buyer treats the situation.

"As I shared the other night, most people experience two significant pitfalls with finances. The first is that they overextend. This occurs when monthly obligations meet or exceed their monthly earnings. In essence, they are spending more than they are making. I have seen this time and time again with my clients, and it seems that you are living it right now. The second financial hazard I have seen many times with my clients occurs when they don't have adequate savings to address unexpected events. I could probably state this more simply by just saying that the problems arise when people don't have enough savings, period. In reality, there are always going to be unexpected events in life. So instead of saying that there are those that don't have adequate savings for unexpected events, it can be more simply said that they don't have enough savings. You haven't experienced this yet. But if you don't make some changes, you'll just think the situation you are in now is bad."

Stan was being very gentle with me, but I certainly felt like I was reliving a conversation that I'd had with my father after having a little too much fun during my first semester of college.

He continued, "Knowing this, it is critical that people understand some concepts related to budgeting and spending money before they borrow money. That might sound somewhat simplistic, but I'm shocked at the number of people who don't put much consideration into it. They don't ask questions like these: Do we really need this right now? Is it possible to save up for it and not borrow to buy it? If it is something that we need to borrow for, what can we do to plan for debt? These are just a few of the questions I wish people would ask more consistently before just doing what everyone else does and adding debt to their lives.

"Here is a little secret. Despite my profession as a mortgage loan officer– someone in the business of making loans–I am almost diabolically opposed to debt. I loathe credit card debt. Car loans and student loans are not far behind. Scripture teaches that the borrower is a slave to the lender."

There was that same quote!

He added, "Even if I have just borrowed money from a buddy to buy a sandwich for lunch, something that I have to admit happens too regularly because I don't normally carry around much cash, I feel an overwhelming sensation to pay that money back immediately. I just don't like that feeling of owing money to someone. Admittedly, I spend a lot of time analyzing my financial situation on a monthly basis, making sure I stay on top of what is coming in and going out. I learned a lesson a long time ago about being in the lifeboat – you can't help others get in unless you are in it. If I can't keep my financial house in order, how would I expect my clients to do the same? The day my savings exceeded my mortgage loan was a banner day that my wife and I celebrated. I've learned that using a mortgage loan can be one of the pillars to someone's overall financial success if used correctly, and I do my best to use the platform I've been given in my clients' lives to coach them on all aspects of how to best handle their finances.

"I don't have a personal story of financial disaster and recovery like many do. I could give you countless examples of people, both locally and historically, who have gone from rags to riches. And in many cases, it was almost an overnight event. But my story of winning, over the long haul, probably resembles a lot more folks than the rare stories of rags to riches. While I get motivated hearing about folks who come up with a great idea and go from paupers to princes, I get more stoked when I read about men and women who have learned how to succeed without an immediate cash inflow. Guys and gals like that are financial rock stars! I don't have that exciting 'rise from the ashes' type of story. I've never liked debt, so I've never been in a position to lose it all. Other than my very first car that my wife and I bought together, which was paid off in less than a year, the only thing I've ever borrowed money to buy is a house. I've just sort of plodded along, saving as much money as I could along the way. The reality is that my story probably resembles 99% of the people who I encounter daily.

If we want to have success, particularly financial success, we have to create it in a very methodical way. It takes years of doing the little things well to get there.

"Other than that one-in-a-million person who hits it big as an overnight success story, the other 999,999 of us won't get rich overnight or even over a very short time. It just doesn't typically work that way. And I'm certainly not telling you to set your sights low. One of the beautiful things about living in this country is that anyone, from any background, at any time, has the opportunity to be that next overnight success story. That is truly a remarkable aspect of being an American. But what I'm talking about here is developing a way of life that will promote financial success that comes over a lifetime. Not that it's a problem if you are the one in a million that it happens to overnight, but more important, that you still become financially successful even if you don't hit it big quick. It is a process, not an occurrence. I want you to get the book *The Millionaire Next Door* by Thomas Stanley and commit to reading it over the next month. You will understand a lot more about this concept when you read that book.

"My parents taught me at an early age that the bank would actually pay me money if I put my money into a savings account. Granted, I knew very little of how the banking system worked, and it certainly wasn't a significant amount of money, but I loved earning $3 to $5 a year for every $100 that I put there. To me, it was free money – and I live by the saying 'If it's free, it's me!' From the time I was a nineteen-year-old sophomore at the University of Tennessee in Knoxville, I was mesmerized by personal finance and how critical it was to master the concept. I loved studying the markets and seeing how everything was intertwined among business, politics, and human nature. As my studies continued, so did my desire to not only understand how behavior, culture, and psychology impact personal financial decisions but also be involved in some type of career that allowed me to help people succeed in this area of their lives. I understood very early on that every decision ultimately has a financial impact. I also learned that it was more important to focus on how to save money versus how to spend it.

"That is pretty much all you need to know about me. I just wanted you to know enough that I could entice you to take me up on an offer."

I had no idea where he was going with this, but I was all ears. I was in from the moment I heard about Stage 1 and had a burning desire to get out of it.

Stan looked me straight in the eye and asked, "How would you like to tag along with me as I meet with clients over the next couple of weeks? I know you have a job and we'll have to work our schedules together, but I think meeting some of my clients and learning about their situations will help you with the momentum you are going to need to change your situation."

I was so excited I could hardly contain myself. Trying to be cool and composed, I nodded and said, "That sounds fantastic. I would love it."

"Well, I know it's short notice, but I'm giving a presentation at a high school on Wednesday morning and would love for you to tag along. It is first thing, so we should be done by 9:00."

I simply asked, "Do you want me to meet you here or at the school?"

"You are welcome to ride with me," he said. "I'll see you here at 7:00." We shook hands, and I was out the door.

Stan was setting the stage for me, and he knew it. To this day he says that he had no idea that he would wind up hiring me. He just told me that he sensed something unique in me, and he knew he could help me. That was his intention, to help me. But really, it was more than that. It was who he was.

What I learned from my first meeting with Stan:

1. *If I want the results of my life to be more positive, I have to live differently than my friends (well, at least the friends who are currently influencing me).*
2. *All purchases, particularly significant ones, need to be planned out from a financial standpoint.*
3. *Never borrow money without a specific plan as to how I'm going to pay it back quickly.*
4. *Having financial success and ultimate freedom is a lifelong pursuit.*

THE BASICS OF SAVING AND SPENDING

I called Stan's assistant, Josh, on Tuesday afternoon and got him to tell me Stan's favorite morning beverage. The next morning I showed up at My Home Mortgage with two cups of caffeine delight, ready to take a little road trip. As we drove over to Fairmont High School, he told me that he usually loved speaking to groups about finance, but this morning's talk would be a little different. He would be walking the same hallways that he had walked some thirty years before. I knew he was going to speak to a group of high school students, but I just realized that we were going to Stan's old high school.

It was early February, and he told me that he could still remember many scenes from the spring semester of his senior year. That semester was probably one of the most fun five-month spans in his lifetime. On our drive, he told me about some of his memories of playing ball, having lunchroom conversations, playing practical jokes, taking spring break, and meeting the girl who was the love of his life. I could tell that it was bringing back a diverse group of feelings and emotions. He said, "Little did I realize while going through that time period that it would be one that I would look back on as having some of my fondest memories."

He was out of town during his thirtieth high school reunion a few years back and had not been on the campus in well over a decade, but when his buddy Matt asked him to talk to the group of seniors that Matt was teaching this semester, Stan jumped at the opportunity. As we drove onto the campus, he glanced over at the football field and told me he had been the quarterback of the team that had been the first for Fairmont High to make it to the state championship game. He said, "It was a heartbreaking loss to a team out of Memphis, and I remember crying with my teammates as we sat in the locker room after the game and recounted our near miss that day."

As we pulled into the parking lot, he pointed to a couple of telephone poles and told me about a prank that he and some buddies had pulled on their basketball coach. The two telephone poles were still standing where they had wedged their coach's little Datsun 260Z in between them. He smiled as we got out of his car. I could tell that he had some good times here.

Stan also gave me the lowdown on Matt. Matt taught math at Fairmont and had been teaching a spring semester class designed to help seniors be better prepared for life in college and beyond. Matt was actually the younger brother of one of Stan's best friends from the same high school. Stan had helped Matt and his wife, Missy, with the mortgage financing for their first home and the home that they now lived in. It was during the process of buying their first home that Stan shared with Matt the importance of budgeting and saving. While certainly not a monumental concept, it was presented to Matt in a way that he had never before heard. It was eye-opening at the time and ultimately became life altering. By living out the simple model he learned almost twenty years earlier, Matt and his wife, Missy, were able to live with something so many of Matt's friends wanted, and that was freedom from financial burdens. And they did it without making a lot of money.

The students in Matt's class were very bright. Matt had been given the flexibility of deciding who could be in the class, and he had chosen kids who excelled not only with numbers but in all aspects of their education. Before Stan stepped foot on campus, Matt had prepped the class on the monumental difference that Stan's advice had made in Matt's life. Because of the class's admiration of Matt, Stan had their immediate attention the moment Matt introduced him.

Stan told me later about how much this caught him off guard. Initially he thought that he was going to have to do something to get their attention. He had a couple of jokes at the ready but quickly realized they weren't needed. After a joke or two, he figured that he would start out with the old "if you fail to plan, you plan to fail" routine and talk to them about the importance of goal setting and laying out a plan of action that would lead to success. He could clearly tell, based on the unmistakable focus in the room and some pre-class conversation with a couple of the students who arrived early, that Matt had made this point very clear throughout the first month and a half of the semester, and they were well aware of the benefit of setting goals. So Stan decided to jump right in and drive his main point home.

Stan told the class that he was going to ask a simple question that required a quick answer. He began, "You have an option in a hypothetical scenario. Right now would you rather be given $1 million that you get to keep or a penny that doubles in value every day for the next thirty days?"

He gave them about five seconds to think about it and asked for hands to be raised by all who wanted the $1 million right now. Twenty-seven of the thirty hands in the classroom went up. He then allowed the remaining three to raise their hands as they had obviously chosen to take the penny that doubled every day. Ironically, but in typical high school fashion, only one of the three remaining hands went up. Ignoring the two dissenters, Stan asked the one who raised his hand why he chose the penny that doubled every day. The young man replied, "I'm not sure, but I figured if that many people assumed that taking the $1 million was the better option, there had to be some kind of trick. So I went the other way."

Stan immediately responded with an almost thundering voice, "How right you are, my friend! You may have backed into the answer without actually considering the numbers, but you have hit on a concept that is going to serve you well in the future! What is your name, young man?" Stan jotted a quick note to himself on a notepad that he kept in his pocket.

"Jake, sir," the young man replied.

Stan nodded and turned his attention back to the class and asked if they understood the concept of compound interest. Less than half the class raised their hands claiming to understand this concept. Stan told them that Albert Einstein said, "Compound interest is the eighth wonder of the world. He who understands it, earns it; he who doesn't, pays it." He continued, "Explained simply, compound interest is interest earned on interest. You invest $1 and earn 5%, you have $1.05 at the end of the year. The next year, assuming you earn 5% again, the interest earned is not just on the initial $1 invested; it is also earned on the 5¢ of interest earned the year before. So you are earning interest on the initial investment of the $1 PLUS earning interest on the 5¢ of interest you earned the year before. It may not seem like much, but it adds up."

Stan went back to Jake and asked him, "Since you went against the crowd, you are obviously hoping that starting with a penny, but doubling the value every day, puts more in your pocket than $1 million, correct?" The young man replied with an affirmative answer, so Stan asked him, "How much more than the $1 million that everyone else got were you hoping to have by starting with the penny?"

Jake said, "I'm still not honestly sure I chose wisely, but maybe by the direction you are going, it actually will be a little more. I have no idea."

Stan asked, "Would you be happy if I told you it was double what everyone else got?"

The young man let out an "oh yeah!"

Stan then said, "Well, if you are happy with double, you are going to be thrilled to know that your penny grew to almost $11 million by the thirtieth day." The class was amazed, and Stan paused a moment to let that sink in.

His desire with this analogy was twofold. First, he wanted to get the students' minds engaged in the power of saving money, and second, he wanted them to start embracing the fact that money could actually work for them and not vice versa. He understood that the culture of the students growing up in that era was all about spending. It was everywhere you turned. If anything, it has gotten worse. Every media outlet that young people are engaged in is advertising to them about how to spend their money. Nowhere is there a reinforcement of the importance of *not* spending money. Ask a teenager today, and she will be able to list all the latest fashion and technological updates. But if you ask her what a mutual fund is and how compound interest works for those who start at an early age, you will get a deer in the headlights stare. That was certainly the case for me.

Stan turned back to Jake and said, "I want to go back to something that was an underlying reason behind Jake's decision to go the penny route. He really wasn't sure that he was going the right direction. He simply decided that if everyone else was so sure that they had the right answer, because it was the easy decision, there might be something a little deeper that was worth considering. He used an instinct that is not too familiar to young people or their elders for that matter. He chose the path less traveled, and as Robert Frost once said, 'Two roads diverged in the wood, and I–I took the one less traveled by, and that has made all the difference.' Certainly if we had been talking about real money, the decision Jake made would have made a significant difference. He made that decision because a little voice inside him told him that something just wasn't right about everyone else so easily jumping in and going down the path that seemed more easily rewarding." He shot a little glance over at me. Not enough for anyone in the room to notice, but he wanted to make sure that I got the message.

At this point, Stan paused again, giving the young people a chance to consider their decision process. He said, "We'll get back to some specific strategies related to saving versus spending and the huge importance that it plays. And if we don't have time, I'm sure Mr. Matt will be covering the topic with you soon. But first, I want to ask you a question. And know that the answer is my opinion, but I want you to consider what you think it might be. In terms of money, what do you think is the biggest lie told to our society?"

After a moment, several hands went up, and the students had great responses. For example, "Going to college is critical to getting a great job." "My parents will be able to support me until I am able to support myself." "Buying a new car is the best route to go when buying a car." Stan's favorite, given in a manner that Stan guessed was to get a rise from him personally was this: "Everyone should buy a home."

But then his buddy Jake came through for him again. Jake said, "I think the biggest lie we get is that we should buy stuff we want even if we can't pay for it right then."

Stan got off the stool he had been sitting on and gave Jake thundering applause. It really caught the kids off guard. "Once again, my young friend, you have answered wisely!"

He continued, "Would it surprise you if I told you that according to the Federal Reserve, there is approximately $865 billion in credit card debt in the United States? That is an average of more than $7,000 per household – and if you only consider the households that actually have credit card debt, that number grows to more than $15,000 per household. Does that not astonish you? That means that if you take every household in the country, on average, each has over $7,000 worth of stuff that they bought but couldn't pay for when they bought it."

After gazing at the flabbergasted looks of the students, Stan asked them, "At what point do you think it became okay to buy stuff that couldn't be paid for when it was purchased?" It was a hypothetical question, and Stan wasn't really looking for an answer. Quite frankly, he didn't know the answer, but he knew that even if there wasn't a specific point in time that The Great Lie—something Stan had started calling this mind-set—became culturally acceptable, it was certainly now told to every consumer in the country.

The class agreed with Stan that if you looked back over history, particularly to a time when the typical American household didn't have the luxuries that we have now, it certainly had not always been this way. Long gone were the days of one car, one phone, and one television for a family of four. Now, everyone has his or her own phone, and a TV is in every room of the house. It's deemed tragic if there is only one vehicle for a family of two or more.

"Let me ask another question: Why do you think that retail stores put things like batteries, soft drinks, and candy up near the checkout line?"

Once again several hands went up, and he got answers like "it's for the customers' convenience," "the cheap stuff is up front," and "so Moms have to buy it for their kids to get them to shut up," which made Stan laugh.

"You are all on the right track," Stan said. "How many of you have heard advertisements such as 'same as cash' or 'zero down and no interest for sixty days' or 'buy one, get one free' or '0% interest'?" All hands went up. "The reason behind this type of marketing," Stan continued, "is the same as the reason stores put convenience items up near the checkout line. They are enticements to try and get you to buy *now*." He added emphasis to his tone when he said the word *now*. "Whether it is a car or a pack of chewing gum, we are encouraged to buy *now*."

"Can anyone tell me what impulse buying is?"

Several hands went up, and almost everyone was either smiling or giggling.

But before anyone had a chance to answer, Matt jumped in. "We spent an entire class session one day last week discussing this very topic. Everyone understands that impulse buying is simply an unplanned decision to buy a product or a service. We won't go down that rabbit hole again, but please understand that they identify with the concept well. Let's just say," as Matt stood up and started to walk around the room, "that Mandy here buys clothes on impulse." He stopped and placed his hand on her shoulder as she glanced up at him and gave him a sheepish grin.

"Mike over there can't seem to say 'no' to whatever the latest shoe that Nike is selling." As he said this, Mike stuck both his feet in the air to show off his latest purchase – camouflaged running shoes with a fluorescent orange Nike swoosh.

"And Annette, sitting right next to you, gets the jitters if she passes a Starbucks without stopping for her afternoon frapp-lappa-somethingachino." Everyone laughed as Annette nodded her head like a turkey gobbler and said, "Oh yeah!"

"So yes," Matt continued, "we have thoroughly covered the topic of impulse buying and how detrimental it can be to accomplishing financial goals. We also talked about how much easier it is to spend money with a credit card versus paying cash, and the emotional connection that is lost when you hand someone a piece of plastic versus dollar bills."

"Great," Stan went on. "So how do we avoid The Great Lie and live a life that is different from the masses?" He again shot a quick glance my way. "I believe the solution lies with something I shared with Matt many years ago, and it was why Matt asked me to come and talk to you guys today. I explained to Matt many years ago that he could ultimately have everything in life that he wanted, financially speaking, if he would simply structure his spending habits into a manageable arrangement where he took care of the important things first and then lived within the constraints of what was left.

"What I taught Matt was that it was imperative to set aside the first 20% of what he made every month and dedicate that money to both giving and saving. What he would do with that 20% would be where his foundation for financial and personal success would come from. Then simply live on the remaining 80%. For Matt, it was easy to split the 20%. As a Christian, he had always given 10% to his church and other organizations that were doing mission and humanitarian work, both in his local area and across the world. Matt understood by setting aside 10% every month to be saved, he would have a nest egg that would allow him to excel when life presented the need. The challenge for Matt and Missy–the same challenge for anyone else devoted to living this way–was to take control of their expenses so that they could pay everything with the remaining 80%.

"The reality is that the less you can live on, the better. If you could live on 50% of your monthly earnings, you would be a financial rock star. I know many people who have set a goal to earn enough income per month from residual income, that is, earnings from things such as investments or other sources of income that are not tied to their occupation, to cover their monthly expenses. How awesome would it be if you had the freedom and flexibility to know that your bills are getting paid this month whether you go to a job or not? Think for a moment about how you could spend your time, money, and efforts if your bills were paid each month without the need for you to go to a job. That certainly can't happen without hard work and discipline, particularly early on. But what a lofty goal that would be! Your primary and initial target is 80%, though. I suggest starting at 80% because personally I believe it is vital to be able to give at least 10% of what I make every month and save 10% of what I make every month. If I can do more, that is great. But at a bare minimum, it has to be 10% for each of those things. So to do that, I have to be able to pay for all of my other expenses with 80% of my income.

"Does anyone in here run track?"

Two young men sitting next to each other right in the middle of the classroom raised their hands, and one indicated that they both ran cross-country.

"Let me ask you something," Stan inquired as he walked down the aisle of chairs toward them, "What is your goal as it relates to each race you run, particularly as it relates to the race before?"

"That's easy," the young man now directly in front of Stan replied. "We always want to win, but our real goal is to improve on the time from the race before. We want to always be improving."

"What a fabulous answer!" Stan exclaimed. "And so it is with your money. It is a never-ending challenge to do better each month than you did the month before with what you have been given. Make it a challenge for yourself to strive to do better each and every day. Unlike a race, however, there is really only one finish line – and you don't cross it until you leave this world. But every month, really every day, you get the opportunity to improve.

"Because finances play a role in every aspect of life, the first step is to embrace this concept. I'm not talking about developing a life where you are consumed by money, particularly in a manner that you become a hermit or a miser. Money is nothing more than a medium of exchange and should be treated accordingly. But starting with the most basic needs, such as food, water, and shelter, all the way up to the fun stuff like taking vacations, attending events, and ultimately retiring, none of this is obtained without a medium of exchange – your money. So before proceeding further, it is important that you understand that almost every decision you make has a financial implication. There is a trade-off. You obtain your wants and needs by paying for them with the money that you have earned. So the first step is to recognize money for what it is and the significant role it will play in your life. Money is not static. It is constantly moving, and you must decide to make it move in your favor.

"The next step is that you must decide, and I mean you have to make this decision *right now*, whether you are going to be your money's master or you are going to be content to serve it. This sounds like a no-brainer, right? No one really wants to be a slave to anything. But it is amazing how many people will so quickly let themselves become a slave to debt and overspending. What I'm talking about here is really even bigger than one of the largest financial decisions you'll make, such as buying a home. We are talking about a lifestyle. To be successful with your financial affairs, you must determine that you are going to take charge of your finances and be your money's boss. Not the other way around.

"As a society, we have allowed the American Dream to turn into the American Nightmare. There was a time, and it really wasn't that long ago, when people actually saved money to buy things, particularly the big items like cars and home electronics. They just made do with what they had until they were able to save up enough to buy what they wanted. Today, people buy what they want right now and worry about paying for it later."

Then he looked at them out of the corner of his eye and gave an incredulous expression before saying, "I actually had a family member, who is an accountant, tell me, 'It's just not possible to buy a car without taking out a loan, so that is what everyone does.' I cringed when I heard that. How could someone who is as close to me as she is say that to me? Aaaahhhhh!!! It makes me scream. And the problem, as I see it, is that if she believes this, and she is well educated, not just in general, but specifically with numbers, how many others believe the same way? Who convinced us that borrowing for a car, a depreciating asset, is a wise decision? By the way, you do know what *depreciating* means, correct?"

He looked around the room to pick someone who hadn't answered. He selected a young man who was trying to avoid being noticed and called on him even though his hand was not raised. "Young man in the green buttondown, what is a depreciating asset?"

"Well," he replied, "since something goes up in value when it appreciates, I assume that when it depreciates, it goes down in value."

"Correct," Stan complimented him. "Unless it is some type of classic, every car will lose value over time. New cars especially – they can lose up to half of their purchased value in the first three to four years." Very sarcastically, Stan added, "Sounds like a great asset to borrow money against. I get the argument someone might provide that 'I have to have a vehicle to get me where I need to go, particularly to a job.' For someone in that situation, I might make an exception and say that it is okay to take out a loan. But that would only be if the person bought something with a loan that could be paid off in a year or less, and that paying it off fit within the 80% rule as part of his budget, so that the required payment and the extra payment to the loan's principal were included in the expenses that make up 80% of his net income.

"I have one more debt-related topic that I want to discuss with you," Stan said. He then asked the class, "How many of you plan to go to college?"

Not surprisingly, all but a handful of them raised their hands, indicating that they would be seeking degrees at the next level.

He asked, "How are you planning on paying for school?" Before anyone could answer, he asked another question: "Before you answer, do you think there is anything such as good debt, and if so, is debt taken out to go to college one of those good debts?"

Hands started flying up all over the room, but Stan pointed to the young lady who had raised her hand a little timidly and said, "Give me your opinion, young lady. But first, give me your name."

"I'm Katie, Katie Ayers," she said. "I'm already guessing that you won't agree, but I don't think I'll be able to go to school unless I take out student loans. My parents have told me that they will try and help me pay for them when the time comes. They believe in education and think that money borrowed for my school is an investment in my future. So, yes, I would say that sometimes, there can be good debt."

"Okay, I appreciate your answer and your honesty, particularly in light of the fact that you believed so strongly that I would disagree with you," Stan replied. "I believe that your parents are no different than the majority of parents who only want the best for their children. Does everyone agree with, Ms. Ayers?"

Most said they did and that school was just too expensive without the assistance of student loans. I was definitely in agreement with them. I hated paying back my loans, but it was the only way I knew to get through college. There were a few dissenters. Mainly Jake, who simply said, "Being in debt just sucks. I don't want any part of it."

One of his buddies said, "Yeah, but you're getting a full ride, so you don't have to worry about it." I was busy being a fly on the wall, but I could sense the tension in the room about this topic. I could tell that Stan was concerned with their thought process, but I also sensed that he empathized with their situations. I knew from my experience which side of the coin I would have been on had I been in the class.

Stan continued, "Okay, let me ask one other question on this topic. How much money do you think is currently owed by people in the United States for student loans? Keep in mind that the total credit card debt is $865 billion."

The guesses were all over the board. By this time, they had gotten more used to his leading questions and were not going to be taken in by answering anything that seemed like the easy answer. He went to the dry erase board at the front of the room and wrote this figure for them to see: $1,200,000,000,000. Obviously he did it for effect. He knew how smart this young group was and that seeing all of those zeros would be mind boggling to them. He turned back to them and said, "Now that you see this number, knowing what we've already discussed about taking the path that is less traveled, do you still think it is a good idea to borrow money for school? Have you fully bought into the thought process that 'education is just so expensive right now that you have to borrow money to go to school' – and besides, it is 'good debt' since it is going for education?" The class sat silently.

"I'm not telling you what to do here. But I will tell you this. I'm shocked at the number of first-time home buyers who come to me for a mortgage loan but are mired in student loan debt. They are trying to do the right things financially but spend their twenties anchored down by debt so they could get a piece of paper. I'm not discounting the value of the degree and how much it helps in obtaining a good job. Just let me encourage you to seek out every possible alternative before borrowing to go to school. Live at home. Get a job. Get two jobs. Seek out every grant and scholarship possible. Eat noodles and beans for four years if you have to, but don't necessarily eat that combination together!" He grinned when he said this.

"Find a way. And more than anything else, have a plan going into the deal. If you decide that borrowing money for school is the only way, make sure you have an exit strategy. Limit the amount you borrow, and set a deadline for paying off the debt. Avoid the easy path of letting Uncle Sam pay for your education. When you let him do it for you, he owns you."

At this point, Stan glanced up at the clock and realized that he had just a couple of minutes left. He had wanted to talk to them more specifically about budgeting and go over some of the X's and O's related to that, but figured Matt could handle that. Stan finished by thanking them for an incredible opportunity that he had been given to share with them this morning. He challenged them to live life differently from the rest and asked them to commit to a debt-free life – never borrowing for anything unless it was an asset that produced income or an appreciable asset like a home. He dared them to commit to being lifelong savers and daily givers. He also encouraged them to heed the words Matt had taught them and would continue teaching them the rest of the semester.

Matt shook Stan's hand and patted him on the back as every member of the class stood and applauded. Just as they did, the bell rang. If I hadn't known better, I would have thought Stan choreographed that.

The students piled out as Stan and I stayed for a minute to talk to Matt. We were interrupted several times as many of the students insisted on giving Stan high fives before leaving the classroom. Matt looked at me and said, "Stan tells me that you are going to hang out with him some over the next few weeks and that this was your first stop. What did you think?"

I tried to hold back some of my enthusiasm and responded in as matter-of-fact manner as I could, "This was great. I think I probably learned more than anyone in here. I wish I had been in a class like this eight years ago when I was a senior in high school. I'm totally jealous of what they're getting to learn. Thanks so much for letting me tag along this morning."

What I learned from the classroom discussion:

1. *Make money work for me – take advantage of compound interest.*
2. *Credit card debt MUST be avoided. From now on, if I can't pay for it today, don't buy it.*
3. *Don't buy things on impulse – have a plan for how I spend my money.*
4. *Take care of the important things (those that make a difference) in life first – live with a purpose.*
5. *Give the first 10% of what I make, save the next 10%, and live on the remaining 80%.*
6. *I am the boss of my money. It obeys me because I have a budget.*
7. *Make it an internal competition to do better with my finances every month.*
8. *Be different – often the road less traveled is the one that leads to success.*
9. *Student loan debt should be avoided if at all possible – where was this advice eight years ago?*

4

LEARNING TO BE A STEWARD

A S we walked to the car, my head was spinning. I'd been given more ideas about how my finances needed to be handled in two separate one-hour sessions with Stan than I had received in my previous twenty-six years of life. Where had this message been eight years ago when my parents insisted I take out so many student loans to get my degree? Why had none of this really crossed my mind as I was sinking myself in an abyss of debt? What had I been thinking? I was already spending everything I made, and I wasn't making any real money yet. When Stan asked me my opinion of how things went, I didn't know what to say. I knew he was asking me how I thought the presentation to the kids had gone and what they thought, but all I could do was respond with a question, "Why has no one ever told me any of this before?"

He grinned, almost as if to say, "We are just getting started." Then his grin became a chuckle as he walked over and got a closer look at the two telephone poles. I could tell he was pretty proud of himself, but I couldn't tell if it was about the talk he had just given or the memory of his coach's car wedged between those two poles.

Before starting his car, Stan looked directly at me and said, "I'm going to ask you a couple of questions that I think will likely confirm my thought process about how I can help you. Some of what I have to say may come across as a little blunt. Please don't be offended. Remember that you are the one who came to me asking for help. If what I say is a little offensive to you, it is probably a good thing. I've only known you a couple of days, but I already consider you a friend. So any suggestions I make are for your benefit. That okay with you?"

I told him that there wasn't much he could tell me that would hurt my feelings and said, "I'm tired of feeling like a slave."

As he turned the key in the ignition, he asked, "Mike, do you think you're rich?"

I thought he was joking. I had already shared with him how dire my financial picture looked. I looked at him somewhat incredulously and asked, "Are you serious?"

"Let me give you some statistics," he said. "I'm guessing you have never traveled around the world much."

I shook my head. Truth be told, I could count on both hands the number of times I'd been out of the state.

He continued, "If you own a car, you are in the top 6% of richest human beings worldwide. If you make $37,000 per year or more, you are in the top 4% of income earners worldwide. If your family owns a house, you are in the top 3%. Staggering, huh? Now, let me ask you again, do you think you're rich?" He paused but continued before I could answer. "We are living in the richest nation on the planet and at probably the richest period in history. Most of us don't like to think of ourselves as rich. We associate a negative stigma with being rich, regardless of what we have. The funny thing is that our nature causes us to disassociate ourselves from the term *rich*. We think of *rich* as being whoever has more than we do, regardless of how much we actually have. The reality is that compared to just about every other group of people on the planet, we are incredibly rich. We have been blessed in an unbelievable manner.

"My first suggestion to you is to recognize that you're rich. I know, that sounds so funny to hear. The second suggestion I will make in a moment will sound even funnier. I realize that right now, you feel broke and helpless. You feel that way because you don't have proper perspective. You have never traveled to a place where people have to walk two miles daily just to have water to drink. You see only the dire straits that you are in because it is the only thing you are looking at. If you can exit your body for a moment and try to gain a much larger perspective of where you are versus where the majority of our planet's inhabitants are, that alone would give you a much keener perspective of your situation.

"Once you realize you're rich, precisely where you are at this moment in time, you will start to gain a better understanding of your responsibility of being rich. Let me tell you, it has nothing to do with where you live, what you drive, or what you wear. Let's go back to a point I made about Matt and his commitment to living within 80% of his take-home pay. Do you remember why I said that was so important to him?"

I remembered and told Stan, "Yes, it was because he recognized the importance of what needed to be done with the first 20%."

"That is correct," Stan replied. "That is the missing ingredient in your current financial situation." He paused a moment to let that sink in.

It was an awkward silence. I could not disagree and really didn't know what to say. He had summed up my failure in this one sentence. I had been so consumed with myself, wanting to give the appearance of success, that I had ignored the things that mattered, and I'd created a ticking time bomb of my own.

He continued, "While the difficulty for most people and the real work lie in limiting expenses to 80%, that part of the equation only becomes relevant once there is a realization and a commitment to focus on the 20% first. That is where success truly lies. Without the commitment to take out 20% first and use it for the things that really matter, true progress can't be made. Most people live their lives by spending first and saving or giving based on whatever is left over after all other monthly expenses have been paid. When they do that, there typically isn't anything left over. It's why so few people don't have adequate savings and why even more aren't able to truly give anything away. It is the spot in which you have found yourself.

"Matt and Missy learned back then how important it was to have a commitment to savings and what it would mean to their financial success over their lifetime together. Matt already knew back then how important it was to be generous with what God had given him. He told me that he had made a commitment in college before he ever met Missy that he would live out James 1:27, where he was instructed that true religion is lived out by helping those less fortunate. So for Matt and Missy, making the 20% commitment was the focal point and the motivation behind working on the 80% part.

"The best way to make any type of decision is with the end in mind. It is where you have to get. Because Matt realized that for him to accomplish the important things, those done with the first 20%, he gained the motivation to live within the 80%. When he understood that, it became much easier. The two go hand in hand. First the desire and passion have to exist to have a vision of what can be accomplished with the 20%. That gives the motivation to live within the 80% parameter. Then living within the 80% parameter permits the opportunity to give and save the other 20%. It is definitely a tag team.

"The basic message here is to take the first 20% of everything you make and set it aside for savings and giving, before a penny gets spent elsewhere. Then your remaining budget of life's expenses gets addressed with the remaining 80%. If you allow your 'other' expenses to be paid first, psychologically you have lessened the importance of the priority of saving and giving. Like I mentioned to the class about how to avoid financial crisis, having adequate savings is the only consistent way to do that. If having savings is not a priority, where that is being addressed before any other money gets spent, it won't get addressed in the manner it needs to – you will always wind up allocating funds for now as opposed to prepping for later. Once you have figured that out and start applying it, I promise you will start seeing a light at the end of the tunnel."

What he was saying made complete sense, but I had no idea what to do next. There was no way that I could set aside the first 20% of my pay in my current situation. If I did, the creditors would be calling.

I think he sensed that as he added, "I understand that in a situation like yours, it is not just a simple flip of the switch and you can immediately start setting aside the first 20% of your pay every month. You have bills and current obligations that need to be met, and you can't just walk away from those.

"However, I may have a good recommendation for you. I didn't tell you this, but one of the partners of the accounting firm that you work at is a client and friend of mine. Don't worry, I haven't asked him for any background scoop on you. I like getting to know people and forming my own opinions, so that wasn't my point in reaching out to him. Let me ask you something: How much money do you have saved in your company's 401K account? From what my buddy tells me, it is an awesome plan. He told me that you are fully vested after two years of being an employee, and they match 50% of everything you put into the account up to 6% of your base salary." He paused and waited for my answer.

It was a weird sort of pause. Stan wasn't really waiting for an answer because he knew the answer. I mentally noted that in only my second one-on-one conversation with Stan, he had again brought back to mind a conversation I had with my father earlier in life. That conversation occurred when I was ten and had accidentally burned down one of our barns. Similarly, my father asked me a question that he already knew the answer to, but was forcing me to answer, so I would have to verbalize the error of my ways.

I also realized that Stan had taken the time to actually check into this with my employer. That was pretty awesome for him to do that. I admitted to him that saving for something that was so far away had not made any sense to me.

He responded enthusiastically and said, "That's okay. I kind of guessed that before asking the question. This is going to give you a perfect place to start. I want you to sign up for that today as soon as you get back to your office. Even if you only put in 2% or 3% of your pay, it will at least be a beginning for you. The money comes out of your check before it is taxed, and for every $1 you put in, you will automatically have $1.50, which is a 50% return regardless of the investment. At some point, you need to get that total to the full 6% that they match. It's crazy leaving that money on the table. But even 2% is a great starting point."

I agreed and told him I would definitely do that.

"Okay, I know it sounded crazy to you, at least initially, when I explained to you that you're rich," he continued. "Well, my second suggestion for you, after you come to terms with the fact that you're rich, is that you become great at being rich. What I really mean is that you become great at being generous, BECAUSE you are rich. I know this sounds crazy to you with the position that you have currently created for yourself, but hear me out. Once you embrace the significance of what you intend to do with the 20% that you will create in your budget, you will have a new perspective. While your focus will still be on doing the things necessary from a personal perspective to meet your financial obligations, and you continue to have an introspective view, they will be done with a bigger picture in mind. You will have the motivation that you need to restructure your budget because you will have a bigger plan for your money than just living month to month.

"Do you remember earlier in class when I told the kids to treat saving and budgeting like a daily competition to get better? Well, one of the important things to remember about this is that the winner is not the one who has the most money when he dies. That's not the kind of competition I was talking about. I was just challenging them to try and get better every day. You are going to leave this world just like you came in it, with no physical possessions. You have heard the expression 'you can't take it with you,' and that is certainly the case. Ultimately, what is important is what we do with what we have while we are here on this earth. It's not the house you own, your stuff, or even the money you save. The more you are able to accumulate, the more you will have to give away, both during life and after. There is a Bible verse in the book of Matthew that says, 'No one can serve two masters, for either he will hate the one and love the other, or he will be devoted to the one and despise the other. You cannot serve God and money.'

"Don't think that the verses I've been giving you are isolated references in

Scripture about money. Money is referenced more than eight hundred times throughout Scripture. In fact, more than 20% of Jesus's discussion topics revolved around worldly possessions. So please understand that I'm not suggesting that you make a game of how much you can accumulate for yourself. Yes, you are the one doing the saving, but the saving is for a purpose. It is so you can do something spectacular with it. Nothing important is really yours anyway. Your health, talents, abilities, and passion were all given to you by our Creator. What you do with those things is what matters. The game is played by developing a life devoted to living on less so you can save more. The game is ultimately won by what you give away, not what you accumulate.

"In 1 Timothy 6:17-18, Paul tells Timothy, 'Command those who are rich in this present world not to be arrogant nor to put their hope in wealth, which is so uncertain, but to put their hope in God, who richly provides us with everything for our enjoyment. Command them to do good, to be rich in good deeds, and to be generous and willing to share.'

"There are four points that I think the Apostle Paul is making here. The first is not to be arrogant with your wealth. Even if you earn every penny of your wealth through hard work and effort, you are no better than anyone else in God's eyes. The second is not to place your trust in your wealth. While I believe strongly that building up adequate savings is crucial to providing stability and safety for you and your family, no amount of money saved will keep you from dying. We are all going to die, and no amount of money can prevent it. Put your faith and trust in something eternal – not in money. The third point is not to forget that everything you have is a gift to you anyway. Even for the things you work for, you were given the talent and ability to achieve, and you were granted a circumstance that allowed you to accomplish whatever successes you may have. Always be grateful. Last, don't forget that whatever wealth you may have is not for you. If everything you have was given to you anyway, you have no rightful ownership. You are an overseer, a shepherd if you will, of what you have been given. Treat it that way.

"I'm sure you've heard the term *stewardship*. I read a definition of stewardship the other day, and it resonated with me. It read like this: 'stewardship is the acceptance or assignment of responsibility to shepherd and safeguard the valuables of others.' That is exactly what I'm talking about here. Recognize that what you have is a gift, and use it for the benefit of others.

"Here is my next recommendation to you. I would like you to find a charity that helps a specific group of people, one that you would be personally interested in helping, and I'd like for you to start giving them $100 per month. I believe that once you start doing this, you will want to take an even more active role with them, but simply making a nominal contribution to their efforts is a great place to start. I know that these ideas–putting money in your 401K and making a monthly donation to a charity–will be new concepts to you. Also, I realize that there are some significant budgeting changes that you are going to need to make. Sometimes it is important to tear the old structure down so a new foundation can be laid before building again. I see tremendous potential in you, and I believe the things you are going to learn over the next couple of weeks will give you incredible momentum to make the changes necessary in your financial habits."

As we pulled into Stan's parking lot, he said, "I want to tell you one more thing that I think will be relevant to you sooner than you think. Maintain your lifestyle even when your income grows. The longer you can do that, the faster your savings can grow. In other words, if your income grows by 10%, but you maintain a budget of expenses that stays at 80% of your former income, you now have an additional 9% of your income that can be allocated to giving and saving. That may not sound like much. However, you would be nearly doubling the amount you save. In other words, if your net income per month is $3,000 and you have an expense budget of $2,400 (80% of $3,000), where you are giving $300 away and saving $300, and your income grows to $3,300 per month, keeping your expenses at $2,400 will allow you to add an additional $270, assuming you continue to give 10% away, to your savings. Or in your case, you can add the additional money to debt reduction.

"We will get together before the end of the month and discuss your numbers specifically, and I'll help you come up with a plan of action. For now, I want you to see living and breathing examples of my clients and their situations. Speaking of which, any chance you are available Friday morning? Josh just texted me about a client who has asked for a meeting, and it sounds like one that you would definitely want to sit in on."

I had told Stan that early morning meetings were great for me as I could just work a little later on those days. My company allowed me some flexibility with my work schedule as long as I put in a full day. I told Stan that I'd see him Friday morning.

What I learned from the car ride:

1. *I am rich – I need to embrace that fact.*
2. *Generosity is something that needs to be a part of my life.*
3. *The Bible has a lot to say about money.*
4. *Be a steward – everything I have is a gift anyway.*
5. *I have to get a vision for my 20% so that it is my top financial priority.*
6. *Don't change my living habits and expenses when my income grows.*

FIXING A DEBT PROBLEM

L**ISA** Jones had called Stan's assistant, Josh, while Stan and I were at the high school Wednesday morning, requesting a face-to-face meeting with Stan. After only five minutes on the phone with Lisa, Josh realized that their frustration was really more like exasperation. He spent about fifteen more minutes calming her down and getting the scoop on her situation. She and her husband did not want to buy a home at this point. They just wanted advice on how to fix the mess they'd gotten into. Josh went ahead and got their complete application and permission to check their credit, as he knew Stan would need that information to advise them more thoroughly. Since she was close friends with one of Stan's very good clients, Josh rearranged a few things on Stan's schedule so he could meet with Lisa and her husband first thing Friday morning. He had texted Stan while we were visiting Fairmont High, and it had actually been Josh who recommended that I sit in on this one.

I got to Stan's office half an hour early, coffee in hand. Before the Joneses arrived, Josh read Stan the notes he had taken from his conversation on Wednesday morning, and I listened in. They had purchased their home two years ago, about a month after they got married. Ironically, this was a second marriage for each, but the first time either had purchased a home. To get them qualified, their loan officer recommended that they liquidate their 401K to come up with the money for the down payment. They had received a gift for the additional up-front money to cover the closing costs. So minus the retirement account, they had no savings. And with their other debt, primarily credit cards, their monthly debt payments, counting the new mortgage, were still about half of their gross monthly income and closer to 65% of their net. When Steve got laid off from his job five months before meeting with Stan, they didn't have the ability to pay everything. So first the credit cards got skipped, and they were currently two months behind on the mortgage. Lisa shared her situation with a friend, who told Lisa that she needed to see "Stan the Mortgage Man."

Josh kind of chuckled as he read this, and Stan shot him a look. Clearly there was more to that story, but I decided to let it go for the time being. Josh had gotten enough information from Lisa over the phone to have a complete loan application and credit report that he handed to Stan. Just as he finished, Steve and Lisa came in the front door.

After making introductions and obtaining permission from them to have me sit in on their meeting, we all went into Stan's office to discuss the situation. Well, they were going to discuss the situation; I was going to be a fly on the wall and just listen.

Lisa started, "Stan, thanks so much for your willingness to meet with us so quickly. We are really in a bind. We shared with Josh a little on the phone Wednesday about the situation we have gotten ourselves into. I'm sure our credit is shot. We have a couple of bills that haven't been paid in months. And we just made a mortgage payment this week, but until then we had been two months behind with that as well. We figured we were headed for foreclosure and probably bankruptcy. But after looking for several months, Steve was able to land a pretty good job. He will be making the same amount he made on his prior job, so maybe there is a light at the end of the tunnel. We were just caught completely off guard by his layoff, and we have tried our best to survive on my income. Unfortunately it just isn't enough to pay all of our bills."

I immediately remembered what Stan said about problems arising for his clients because of unforeseen circumstances. I was curious to see whether he would be compassionate or stern with his instruction. I guess everyone's story had different variables, but as I quickly learned, they were all basically the same – an unexpected event came up and there was neither the income nor the savings to handle it. While the obvious issue was dealing with the current circumstance, the real problem was created by the lack of preparation for the event.

Somehow he had to get this message across to them because he knew that the only way they would ever truly recover was to take responsibility for their part in this situation. Yes, they felt manipulated by their former loan officer and the job loss worsened the situation, but the bottom line was that the situation was created by Steve and Lisa. It would be much easier to let them play the blame game, but that wouldn't accomplish anything. The reality is that the steps that needed to be taken at this point were the same regardless of how they got here.

Stan knew it would be tough for them to hear, and maybe just as tough for him to relay, but they needed to hear that they were the ones responsible for their mess, and they needed to embrace that concept. It was the only way to give them the motivation to get out of this place and make sure they never got to it again.

He laid their application and credit report on the table in front of them and said, "I have reviewed both your application and your updated credit report. We are going to go through this information methodically. But before we do, I need to know how committed you are to fixing this. I'm probably going to say some things that you do not want to hear and honestly might offend you. Please understand that I want nothing but the best for you, and I want to point you in the right direction. What I'm going to suggest to you won't be easy, and it will certainly not be something that you can accomplish overnight. But ultimately, recovery depends on you and your future actions. Are you willing to do what is necessary to turn this ship around?"

Lisa started to answer, but Steve beat her to it. He said, "Stan, I can't live like this anymore. I'm humiliated that we got ourselves in this position. I'm embarrassed that I lost my job, I'm tired of running from bill collectors, and I want a new direction."

Stan was pleased at hearing this. He could tell from Lisa's reaction that she was neither pleased by Steve's interruption nor was she thrilled with his complete admission of blame. But I could tell that Stan was glad that Steve had gotten to the point of brokenness, and he knew Lisa would need to get there as well if his plan for them had any chance of working. So he looked Steve in the eye and said, "Great, I'm thrilled to hear that. I think I can help.

"The first thing I want us to do," Stan continued, "is take a look at your savings account. From the information Lisa gave Josh, it doesn't appear that there is much money in the account."

Lisa spoke up, "Well, we spent most of our savings on our wedding a couple of years ago. We both came out of short-lived marriages, and we wanted to make a statement when starting our new life together. Then we immediately bought our house, and as I shared with Josh on the phone, we used up the savings we had left, plus some of our retirement, to get into the house. Since then, we've pretty much lived on what we made. So we never really built the savings back up."

Stan said, "I understand that, but you need to understand something very clearly. The only way you will ever be able to avoid circumstances in the future when things don't go as planned is to have an adequate amount set aside in savings to help pay for those types of things. So one of the first things I want to see you guys do is build that savings account back up. You need at least three months, and preferably six months, of monthly expenses saved in a readily accessible savings or money market account. That is the first step to establishing a solid financial foundation. With an adequate emergency fund, you will be able to avoid those unexpected emergencies and have cash ready and waiting to take care of them."

Changing directions for a moment, Stan said, "Now let's talk a little about your spending. To get where we need to be from a savings perspective, we need to first establish a spending budget so that we can make sure you are telling your money where to go each month versus it bossing you around. Does that sound okay?"

They both nodded, so Stan continued, "Okay, looking at the credit report, I see three credit cards to department stores, two regular credit cards, two car loans, a mortgage, another installment loan that I assume is tied to the boat, and I see where Josh listed a monthly child support payment. Does that sound accurate from a liability standpoint?"

Both nodded somewhat ashamedly. "Okay, then what I want us to do next is examine your budget. It is obvious where some of the money is going. Let's talk about the rest. We need to compare what is coming in to what is going out." Stan pulled out a blank sheet of paper and glanced up at them to see what kind of reaction he might get. It had been his experience that most folks in similar situations never took the time to put pencil to paper to see exactly where their money was going every month. It had also been Stan's experience that most people cringed even at the thought of doing a budget – it was almost like saying a four-letter word. It's ironic that people will spend an hour planning a dinner party for Friday night but won't take fifteen minutes to schedule where their money is going that month.

"We are going to make this as simple as possible. From your application I see that Lisa's salary is $55,000 and Steve's new job pays him $75,000 for an annual total of $130,000 or $10,833 per month." He glanced up at them to make sure that he was accurate. When they did not disagree, he went on. "Adding up your debt-related expenses from the credit report, the total is $3,860 per month." He then had them list their other expenses on a monthly basis and concluded, "When we add the rest of the monthly expenses, the total is $6,040.

Looking accurate so far?" They both agreed. "Well, when we deduct the amount Uncle Sam gets, that gross pay drops to about $7,041 per month. Subtracting the expense from the net income leaves you close to $1,000 left over at the end of the month. Does that seem about right?"

Lisa said, "That is probably correct, but when Steve was out of work, that 'end of the month' number had a big negative in front of it."

Monthly Budget

| Gross Income: | 10,833.00 | | |
| Net after taxes: | 7,041.45 | | |

Expenses:		Balance	Value
Mortgage	1,800.00	250,000.00	275,000.00
Boat	450.00	8,000.00	9,000.00
Auto	325.00	12,000.00	12,500.00
Auto	300.00	4,500.00	7,500.00
Visa	250.00	10,000.00	
MasterCard	145.00	4,500.00	
Nordstrom	150.00	3,500.00	
Neiman Marcus	125.00	3,200.00	
Saks	65.00	2,400.00	
Groceries	300.00		
Gas	400.00		
Clothes	300.00		
Entertainment	350.00		
Cable	100.00		
Cell phone	130.00		
Trash pickup	50.00		
Child support	600.00		
Utilities	200.00		
Total Expenses:	6,040.00		

"I know you feel exasperated right now," Stan said. The timid nature of their individual postures made it clear that they were ashamed to have to be so open about their dilemma. He encouraged them, "Hang in there. You have made an incredible first step by asking for help. And I believe we really have something to work with here. You have a lot going for you in your situation, primarily your income. It is fantastic and will really help you get done what is needed here. You are in the top 25% of income earners in the country. And while your credit has suffered, you haven't committed any grave delinquencies such as bankruptcy or foreclosure, and you have no collections, judgments, or charge-offs.

"Most of the people who go through what you've gone through, where there was a job loss for a lengthy time period with no real savings to get by on, have fared much worse than you. Your marriage is still intact, and if anything, you appear to be even stronger as a unit having survived this situation up to this point. So don't lose heart. What we are going to talk about is going to be challenging for you. But I promise if you will stick with it, your marriage will grow stronger, and your lives will be more impactful.

"I teach all of my clients a simple strategy I call the 80% Solution. It sounds grand, but it is really nothing more than this: Give and save the first 20% of your net income, and live on the other 80%. Once that is in place, you work on getting all non-mortgage debts paid off and the mortgage paid down to 80% of the home's value. Pretty simple, huh? You see, when people look back on their lives, the things that were most important to them really had nothing to do with money. They are things like having relationships with God, family, and friends, enjoying the fun things in life, and leaving a legacy. None of that really has anything to do with budgeting!"

Stan paused for effect, but not long enough that either could respond. "Or does it? As strange as it may sound, all of these things are woven together. For example, let's say that one of the most important aspects of your life is that you have a great relationship with your family members. I want you to think of a family member, and it doesn't matter who." He gave them a moment to visualize someone and continued, "Regardless of what specific member of your family you may be thinking of, do you think your relationship is healthier with that person if your finances are in good order, or would your relationship be better while struggling like you are now?"

Steve answered, "That's an easy one! My relationship right now sucks with everyone I know – I don't want to talk to anybody right now!"

"Right!" Stan said. "What if some of your passions in life are things like coaching a ball team, helping at church, or leading a Boy Scout troop? Would you lead them better from a standpoint of financial security or when your finances are crumbling under your feet? What about giving money to those in need–easier when you have control of your finances or when they are out of control? What about how you want to be remembered? Is it easier to focus on that when you are a master of your finances or a slave to them? What about . . ."

Lisa interrupted before Stan could give another "what if" scenario and said, "Stan, you are dead on. I definitely get what you're saying. This may be the simplest way anyone has ever put this to me before. You've hit the nail right on the head. My finances affect everything about me. I've never considered how everything is tied to together like that. But you are right – nothing is working very well in other areas of our lives right now, and it has everything to do with the state of our finances."

"That's right," Stan said, "and while my desire is to help you manage the minutia, or the 80%, where all the bills get paid, my primary goal is to help you with that first 20% and making it a part of your life and ultimately your plan each and every month. The first 20% is where your legacy will be left. The other 80% is simply about living life with limits. Unfortunately since I did not have the pleasure of assisting you with your home purchase, we are going to have to work backward on this to some degree. This is going to be the part that is some-what painful and requires a commitment to living differently as it relates to your budget. But I'm confident you can do it!

"Before we lay out the framework and I give you a couple of recommen-dations, let me start by saying that this is a work in process – for anyone who chooses to go down this path. It's kind of like running a marathon. You don't go out on day one and run twenty-six miles. Even for the runner who has run multiple marathons, it is not an overnight process to get prepared. Depending on your current condition, it may take you weeks or it may take you years to be able to complete that kind of athletic accomplishment. If you are in outstanding condition and love to run, you may be able to run in a marathon in a couple of months. If you are out of shape and would struggle to walk a mile, the time-frame is going to be more significant for you. The point is that there is an end in mind, and that end result is the same for everyone. Regardless of where your journey begins, you can cross the finish line if you are willing to make the effort. So let's get to the heart of the issue."

With that, Stan turned the budget around so that they could see it right side up. "What do you see on here that is out of whack?" he asked them.

"For starters," Steve replied, "we have way too much credit card debt. That is the thing that probably bothers me the most. And based on what you have told us, pretty obvious that we don't have any strategy for saving money."

Then Lisa added, "I'm ashamed that we can't give money to our church or really anything like that, and I know I spend too much money on clothes."

Stan responded, "Wow, you two are tracking right where I was hoping you would go. It is all about priorities. Once the priorities are established, it becomes much easier to establish a strategy. So what would you guys say is your number one priority right now?"

Steve replied, "That's easy – to get out of this mess!"

Lisa nodded in agreement so Stan knew he had their approval to hit home with a couple of huge points.

"Steve," Stan asked, "how often do you use that boat?"

Steve shook his head and said, "I knew you were probably going to go there. Honestly, I do love my boat and have a good time when my buddies and I go out on it. But truthfully, we didn't get out but maybe three or four times last summer. And I really hadn't planned on going out much this year with my job situation the way it has been. But I do really love my boat."

"Yeah, I certainly understand," Stan agreed, "I've got a good buddy who takes my family out on his boat to fish and ski from time to time. So I understand the joy of being out on the water. What about the department store credit cards?" Stan was still looking at Steve when he asked the question, but he had seen from the credit report that the department store cards were all in Lisa's name.

Stan turned to Lisa, raised his eyebrows, and stated somewhat inquisitively, "I'm guessing that you like to dress nicely!"

Lisa ducked her head down like a child caught with her hand in the cookie jar. She even shot a glance at me at this point, which was the first time either had acknowledged my presence in the room.

"It's okay. I'm not trying to beat you up," Stan continued, "but maybe ruffle your feathers a bit. You see, what we need to do is change some priorities – or at least we need to line up some spending habits with what you are telling me are your longer term priorities. The plan is to free up money from certain categories so that we can add it to other, more important categories. But to do that, your action has to follow your priority. In other words to get out of the mess you are in, you have to live differently than the manner you were living while creating the mess. And the bigger the mess, the bigger the change will need to be.

"You told me that you bought the house as soon as you got married and the extent you went to, liquidating retirement and getting money from family, to make that happen. That event is somewhat of an indictment on where you are, or at least were, from a standpoint of priorities. We often call it 'keeping up with the Joneses.' Kind of fitting for you guys, huh?"

I had to chuckle at Stan's reference to their last name. Fortunately for me, they both laughed as well.

Stan added, "It is where your reality is made up by your appearance. It doesn't matter if it is your car, house, boat, or clothes. Those things are more important to you, or at least they have been, than what you are telling me now is important. So you really have to determine your true priorities. If you are ready to become better stewards of the resources you have and make that your priority, I believe I can help.

"For what I'm suggesting to work, we have to rein in the expenses so that they are manageable and confined to 80% of your net income. To make this happen, we have get your spending lined up with the end in mind and then get out of debt. You guys are going to have to strategize on this. And while I encourage you to take enough time to cover all your bases, I also encourage you to start taking action immediately. I'm going to give you a sample plan of action, and you can use it or create your own plan. But it has to be something that you agree on, and that is non-negotiable.

"You have to get radically crazy about eliminating debt, and that must come from the vantage point of doing something more meaningful with your money. You say that priority number one is to get out of this mess – that it is more important than anything else. Is that correct?"

They both nodded, so he went on. "Why? Why is getting out of this mess so necessary? Now that Steve has the new job, you are making enough money to continue to pay your bills and keep living life as you have lived it."

Steve spoke up with determination, never taking his eyes off Stan. "Honestly, we were probably a month away from bankruptcy before I landed this job. I was already prepared for the humiliation that would come with that. We've now been blessed with a second chance and want a way out. We do want so many of the things you have alluded to here. We want to make a difference. We want to take vacations together. We want to retire one day and live comfortably when we do. We want our children to get educations that will help them be successful in what they do. Right now, none of that seems possible."

With this, Stan knew they had the motivation that would be needed, so he went for the jugular. He looked right at Steve and said, "Steve, you gotta sell the boat." Then he immediately turned to Lisa, before Steve could respond, and said, "Lisa, you can't buy any new clothes for the next twelve months, maybe the next twenty-four."

Stan waited for a reaction. They both started squirming in their seats but didn't raise an objection. "Those two things alone would free up $750 in your monthly budget. And if you will limit your entertainment expense to $150 per month, that will free up another $200. I know that will be tough, but you can still have a lot of fun on $150 per month. This may sound a little crazy, but I know where you live, and I happen to know that the trash/recycling center for our county is only two miles from your house. It's time to start taking your own trash out instead of having it picked up for you. That frees up another $50 and puts us at an even $1,000 immediately freed up that we can add to the $1,000 that you already have expendable.

"I know doing these things isn't comfortable. But let's be honest. What I'm saying isn't really even crazy. If you want to get crazy, there are several other things that you can do. You can get rid of cable television. You could sell a car. Heck, you could sell both cars. Driving older models, even those that might need a little more maintenance than your newer models, will save you a ton of money. No car payments would save you another $775 per month. Heck, you could even carpool together to work and eliminate almost half of your gas bill. What about stuff lying around your house that you don't use or need? Ever thought about a garage sale? Electronics that are past the usefulness stage for you are almost always still useful for someone else and can be easily sold. And once you sell that boat, I'm sure there are plenty of accessories that can be sold as well. My point here is that my initial suggestion will free up an immediate $1,000 in your monthly budget if you don't do anything else. But if you are willing to get really radical about it, I'm sure you can figure out ways to free up more money each month and creative ways to earn more money. The things that Steve described earlier are all obtainable. But they'll never happen unless you make them happen. And there is no better time to start than now." He could see the wheels spinning in their heads.

Steve blurted out, "There is a community garage sale going on in our neighborhood in two weeks. In just a couple of minutes, I've already thought of at least five big-ticket items that we can unload!"

"That's the kind of creativeness I'm talking about!" Stan congratulated him. "Now that we've figured out a way to save $1,000 by doing some of the easy things, let's add that to the $1,000 surplus in your budget and talk about what to do with the $2,000 that you have created for yourselves by doing some of the easy things. You can discuss this with each other and figure out what goes first as far as paying stuff off, but let me give you something else to think about. The way you avoid this type of an emergency in the future is by having funds set aside that can be drawn from in a time of crisis, like a job loss.

"The first thing I want you to do is set up a temporary emergency fund. I call it temporary because it will get you started on developing a full-fledged emergency fund. It will give you some security for the time being, but not be where we need it to be long term. For the first three months after selling the boat and doing the other things I've suggested, I want you to put every bit of that into a savings account that you are not going to touch. That will give you $6,000 in the account, which is enough to cover a full month's worth of expenses. We'll grow that more down the road, but I want you to have that there in case something drastic happens. I don't want your debt reduction plan to go sideways by an unexpected emergency.

"Once you have the $6,000 in place, it's time to go after the debt. Normally I'd say go after the credit card debt first, as it is likely to carry the highest rate of interest, particularly since your credit is so tarnished. And there are two main schools of thought to paying off the credit card debt. The first would be to go after the credit card with the highest interest rate. Pay it off, and then go to the next highest rate card until they are gone. That is the most intellectual route for paying off debt. That is saving you the most money because you are getting rid of the debt that costs the most first. The other method I'd suggest is to pay off the credit cards with the smallest balance first. Once the first one is completely paid off, you go to the next card that has the smallest balance and continue from there in that order. That gives you a lot of momentum as you are seeing the balances disappear quicker, and it gives you motivation to continue your efforts until everything is gone. You with me?"

They both agreed, so he went on, "It doesn't really matter to me how you go about paying the cards off as long as you have a plan and stick to it. However, in your case, I'm going to make one small modification. This suggestion comes with the assumption that you are not going to immediately sell your cars."

Steve interrupted and said, "We may do just that. I know I can get by on a less expensive car." He glanced over at Lisa as he was talking, and it was clear that she was not as excited about the prospect of giving up her car.

"Well, that decision would certainly springboard you farther along the path of being debt free, but for now, we'll operate under the assumption that you are keeping the cars. One of your car loans has a $4,500 balance and carries a $300 monthly payment. I'm going to suggest that you pay that loan off first. Assuming it takes you three months to get your savings where it needs to be, you would be able to wipe the car out in month six if you apply all the extra discretionary income to the car balance. That would give you an additional $300 that you can add to the $2,000 to continue paying debts off. So in month six, you pay the car off and use the other $1,500 to pay on the Saks card. In month seven, pay off the Saks card completely and apply the remaining $1,400 to the Nordstrom's card. In month eight, you have $2,365 to work with (since Saks is gone) and $2,100 left on Nordstrom's. Bye-bye, Nordstrom. At this point, go celebrate! Go out to a nice dinner, and buy yourself something fun! You will have done an amazing job up to this point, so commemorate the moment.

"Now with no Nordstrom or Saks, you have a little over $2,500 to work with monthly. Over the next three months, you will have enough to pay off both Neiman Marcus and MasterCard. Those balances are $7,700, but the payments will come down some as you pay the balances down each month. So at the end of eleven months, you have paid off all credit cards but Visa and have $2,785 to work with each month in paying off the rest. It's time to go after the last card. In four more months, you have Mr. Visa paid off, adding another $250 to your total attack fund – which, by the way, is now over $3,000.

"Don't stop here. You are on a roll. With $3,000 per month to work with, you can pay the other car off in four more months. So in nineteen months you are out of debt! You will have freed up a total of more than $3,300 that you can now put in savings for the next five months. Adding that total to what you saved the first three months, your savings will be at $22,500. And in the process, you will have reduced your necessary monthly expenses to $4,230. So you now have a more fully funded emergency fund, equivalent to over five months of monthly expenses and no debt other than the mortgage. How much freedom do you feel just knowing what your life is going to be like two short years from now? Is that not amazing?"

I was amazed at the change in their countenances and the positive expressions on their faces. Steve and Lisa could hardly contain themselves. They were ready to go into full attack mode, and Stan could not have been happier to see their excitement. He said to them, "I can see that you are excited, and I'm excited for you. It is going to be a challenging two-year period, but I can't wait to visit with you again twenty-four months from now and toast your success. Whether you follow the plan I've laid out for you or come up with a strategy of your own, I know you are going to be successful. I'm putting you down on my calendar exactly two years from today, and we are going to visit again. Before you leave, do you remember what I told you was the most important part of the 80% Solution? It's not the 80% - which is what we've been talking about for the last fifteen minutes . . ."

Steve interrupted, "Yeah, it's that first 20% that makes a difference."

"You are dead on," Stan confirmed. "That is where you make your mark and leave your legacy. By getting to the point that you are going to be in two years, you will have reduced your expenses not just to 80% of your net income, but to 60% of your net income. So you will have more than just 20% to work with as you begin each month. You will be able to start saving like you have never saved before. And the difference you will be able to make with your generosity will be literally life changing. That is what we are going to focus on the next time we meet.

"The other thing we will discuss at that point is getting your mortgage loan paid down to an amount that is no more than 80% of the value of your home. That is another huge piece of the financial puzzle that we'll discuss when I see you again in two years. We also didn't talk about your credit, which I know you are aware is completely shot right now. However, following the plan of paying these debts off and paying all of your bills on time will have a dramatically positive effect on your credit rating. So when we meet again, I want to hear all about your success, as well as the plans you have for using the money that you have freed up in a life-changing way. And we'll dig into the rest of the strategy. You are welcome to call me anytime along the way."

With that, Steve and Lisa literally skipped out of Stan's office. Stan asked me to sit tight for a minute while he grabbed a water bottle and dialed a buddy from his cell phone.

Stan had returned an email from his friend Fred Simmons the night before and promised Fred that he would call him in between his morning appointments. Fred was a savvy businessman and had been a friend of Stan's for a long time. His request was actually a bit unusual. He requested that Stan meet with his daughter and discuss with her the importance of owning a home. According to Fred, his daughter was very intelligent but also not very willing to listen to his instruction. Stan agreed to set up a meeting with her and confirmed my availability first thing the following Tuesday. He expected this would be another good meeting for me to sit in on and told me, "If she is anything like her father, you and I will both be in for a treat."

Stan had about ten minutes before his next appointment, so he asked me, "What do you think of Steve and Lisa's situation?"

"Well," I responded, "I'm amazed at how much debt they allowed themselves to get into, particularly with the income they were making. I understand that Steve was out of work for a while, but they had car loans and a boat loan, and I bet that she had department store debt long before he lost his job. I'm sure the other credit card stuff got worse with the job loss, but I'm pretty confident that they were not in great shape even before that. Is their situation unusual, or is that something you see all of the time?"

"I'd like to say this is an isolated case," Stan responded. "But unfortunately, I see folks in similar condition all the time. Granted, the amount of debt may not be as much. But a lot of times it is related to the amount of income. The more people make, the more comfortable they feel borrowing money for things that don't last. As their income levels increase, so does their spending. They don't give a lot of thought to the fact that their income could drop significantly or altogether, so they don't bother to set anything aside to prepare for that possibility. Then when life happens, they are not ready for it. Steve was dead on. Another month or two and they were going belly up from a financial perspective."

I agreed and told him, "I also was quite impressed at how you were able to so quickly give them a game plan and persuade them to put a plan in place and lay one out for them that was simple to understand and follow."

Stan grinned and said, "That's what I do. Honestly, their situation was pretty easy to diagnose and develop a strategy to deal with it. It is much more difficult for people who don't make the kind of money that they make. Truthfully, if they get really motivated and Steve follows through with selling some of the extra toys they have, they can accomplish their goals in even less than the two-year plan I gave them."

With that, we shook hands, and I headed to my job. This morning had been very interesting.

What I learned from our meeting with the Joneses:

1. *Life happens — be prepared.*
2. *Own up to my situation — I created it; I've got to be the one to fix it.*
3. *An emergency fund is non-negotiable — three months to start, but having six to twelve months of monthly income saved is better.*
4. *Everything, even my family relationships, is impacted by my finances.*
5. *The 80% Solution is a process, not an occurrence.*
6. *It all starts with creating a budget and limiting expenses to 80% of net income.*
7. *My priorities will drive my budget (spending, saving, and giving).*
8. *Have a plan for paying off debt — there are different ways to do this, but the key is to map it out and stick to the plan.*

Rent versus Own

I spent most of the weekend going over all the notes I'd taken on my first few encounters with Stan and could not wait until Tuesday. Stan had already lined up two more appointments for me to sit in on later in the week, and I was anxious to learn more. As I had done the mornings before, I got to Stan's office half an hour early Tuesday morning after stopping to get coffee for everyone.

I was in Stan's office with him when Josh brought Janis in and introduced her to Stan. Janis Simmons was the daughter of one of Stan's longtime clients, and Stan agreed to meet with her and discuss the benefits of homeownership. From what Janis's father, Fred, had said, he and Janis had a great relationship but tended to butt heads when it came to many of Janis's decisions related to her life's direction. Janis was stunning in appearance and personality. It was obvious to me, from her business dress and professional mannerisms, that Stan was talking to someone who had her act together. She had just turned thirty but had never owned a home. According to her dad, she liked renting and not having the responsibility of owning a home. He couldn't get her to understand that she was just wasting money by not buying a home. Stan didn't agree to talk her into anything, but he did say that he'd be happy to meet with her and discuss the situation.

Josh told Stan that he'd just gotten her application information and would be back shortly with a copy of the application and the credit report.

"Great, thanks," Stan said and then turned to Janis, who had just sat down. "So, Ms. Simmons, your dad tells me that he can't convince you that buying a home would be the best thing for you."

"Well, first of all," she replied, "you need to understand that unless I do everything exactly like he does, then I'm doing it wrong, at least according to him. I love him and admire him greatly, but I'm still waiting for him to understand that not everyone has to do things the way he does for them to be right. And I never told him that I thought renting was smarter than buying. It's just a lot easier. I'm pretty confident I could buy. You'll see in a minute, when Josh brings you my credit report, that my credit is great. I also have the down payment saved and don't really have any other debt. I just don't want the responsibility that goes with being a homeowner."

Stan chuckled at this and said, "Ms. Simmons, I certainly understand your point – both about your father and where you are with renting versus buying. I do believe that homeownership is one of the keys to your overall financial health, and I probably agree with your father that paying rent, when you don't have to, is a waste. But I also understand you having no desire at this point for the commitment of time and resources that owning a home brings. I'm not going to try and convince you that you need to buy a home right now. We are actually going to look at the benefits of both owning and renting as well as the downsides of each. You can decide when we are done which makes more sense for you right now.

"I think the list of reasons for why people should rent, or do rent, versus buying is pretty easy. I'm going to write them down for you, and we will discuss each in detail. It probably looks something like this":

1. They can't qualify for a loan – specifically, they can't come up with a down payment.
2. They don't want to be strapped with a mortgage and the responsibility that comes with having that kind of debt.
3. They don't want to worry about values dropping.
4. They don't want to deal with maintenance time and cost (fixing stuff up and doing yard work).
5. They feel the buying and selling process is too expensive.

"Conversely, the reasons people buy a home might look something like this":

1. They have to live somewhere anyway, so they might as well get ownership rights and have something they can call their own.
2. They want a hedge against inflation. In other words, rents historically go up. However, once a mortgage is in place, particularly a fixed-rate mortgage, the payment for principal and interest stays the same.

3. They want the tax benefit of being able to deduct the mortgage interest.

4. They want the forced savings that paying a mortgage provides. Every payment provides a principal component that steadily pays the loan down, building up equity.

5. They realize that buying a home is a leveraged investment if they have a loan. The house goes up in value the same regardless of whether there is a loan or not. The leverage of a loan allows a higher return because the increase in value provides a greater return due to less invested initially.

"I wrote these down for you mainly so you would understand the benefits of homeownership. But I also want you to understand why people don't buy homes. Honestly, there are legitimate reasons not to buy, but some people are better suited to rent. I know you have said that you don't want the commitment of owning a home, and I'm guessing that some of that, in addition to not wanting to commit, is just a product of being busy and not wanting to feel like you are settling down." Janis nodded without saying anything. She was very attentive to what Stan was presenting to her.

Josh came in with Janis's credit report and application. After a two-minute review, Stan confirmed what Janis had said about her credit. He also told her that based on her income and minimal debt totals, she could easily qualify for a mortgage payment that was quite a bit more than she was paying in rent.

Stan then continued the discussion on why people rent. "Most people can't pay cash for a home and need a home loan. To do that, they have to be able to qualify for the loan. For many, credit can be an issue. However, what I've found to be the biggest issue, primarily for first-time home buyers, is that they do not have the funds necessary for the appropriate down payment. They live paycheck to paycheck and have not maintained a budget that allows them to save the type of money that is needed to buy a home. So for those people, it's not that they shouldn't own or that they don't want to, it's simply that they can't. For most of those types, I can coach them on how to better manage their finances and teach them how to save money. It may take a little more time, particularly for some versus others depending on how complicated their situation is, but those situations are usually workable. This is clearly not an issue for you.

"At the other end of the spectrum, from the people who want to buy but can't, are the types who are primarily fearful of owning a home and the responsibility that comes with it. They are scared to have a significant debt, like a mortgage, or they are afraid of what home values might do. I certainly understand both thought processes. Some folks are still pretty old school and just don't want to be in debt. Ironically, despite the business I'm in, I'm pretty opposed to debt. Yet I think I can make an adequate argument, which I'll share with you in a moment, as to why mortgage debt is acceptable and makes sense. But I get the fact that some people just don't handle owing money very well. It is one thing to owe money each month for a rent payment, but it is quite another to owe every month for something that may not be paid off for thirty years. Others are fearful that home values could fall. That is a justifiable fear and one that has to be analyzed before making such a significant purchase. My guess is that either or both of these could be issues for you."

She nodded and Stan continued, "Then there are those who don't want the lifestyle of owning a home, or they just have a lifestyle where homeownership doesn't make sense. We all know people like this. It could be the guy who throws a pool party at his apartment every Saturday or the woman who travels all week on her job. One doesn't want to give up his lifestyle, and the other has a lifestyle that is not as suitable for owning and maintaining a home. There are also those who don't want to deal with the maintenance and hassle issues, like yard work, of owning a home. You may fit in that category as well. They would much rather live in an environment where they know that their lives are free of that type of additional responsibility and stress. And finally there are those who move around a lot, and the expense of buying and selling is more than they can make up, even in an environment where home values are moving up. I understand these types and probably agree with them as much or more than any other type of person who doesn't find homeownership suitable for himself. It probably doesn't make sense to buy a home if there is a tendency or track record of moving around a lot. The expenses of buying and selling outweigh the other benefits."

Janis spoke up at this point: "I think I definitely fit into the category of simply liking the lifestyle that renting gives me. I also don't like the idea of having the debt that goes along with buying a house. Obviously I don't have the savings to pay cash, but the thought of borrowing that much money really makes me feel uneasy."

"I understand," Stan said. "Again, I'm not going to try and talk you into buying a home, but I do think we need to look at reasons people buy and discuss some of the benefits. Personally, I believe that when done properly, owning a home can not only be the place you desire to live your life and raise a family, but it can be the backbone of a financial strategy that supports your overall financial health. Everyone has to live somewhere, right?"

Janis shrugged and nodded her head.

"Knowing this," Stan said, "why not make where you live contribute to the big picture? When you own a home, you have a place that you can rightfully call your own. Where, within reason, you can do what you want, how you want, and when you want without concern of what the owner of the home might think. You are the owner. There is a psychological significance that we equate with being a homeowner that isn't satisfied in any other way.

"I realize that the psychological benefit of homeownership is a little more irrelevant to you. But there is more to it than just the feeling of significance owning a home provides. There are also some very important financial considerations. Over the long term, the purchase of a home is a great hedge against inflation, particularly when a loan is involved. Homes typically appreciate over the long term at a rate of somewhere between 3% and 4%. The same is true with the cost of rent; it goes up as well. Granted, rental rates have not risen nearly at the same pace as housing, but they have definitely gone up. According to the United States Census Bureau, rental rates rose on a national basis from $71 per month to $602 per month between the year 1960 and 2000 (based on the median rental rate). During that same time, the median home value rose from around $17,000 to about $169,000. The point is that like home prices, rental rates rise. Assuming you buy a home and take out a fixed-rate mortgage, your payment is locked in. Granted your taxes and insurance can go up. But the amount you pay for the principal and interest will stay the same. So as opposed to paying rent, where the cost will continue to rise, you will have a locked-in payment on your mortgage and have effectively hedged yourself against the inflation of rising rental prices.

"The second part of that is pretty clear. Because home values tend to rise over time, you are gaining equity, or increased value for the home you own, by simply living there. Again, assuming you have taken out a fixed-rate loan, the payment you make each month has a principal and interest component. So while you are paying interest on the loan each month, and know that the significant part of that payment is interest in the early going, you are still paying a portion to the principal balance of the loan, thus paying it down little by little each payment.

And because you are paying down the loan balance with every payment, the loan gets smaller. If that is happening while the value is increasing, your equity is growing in both directions. For example, if you take out a thirty-year fixed-rate loan at 5% for $200,000, you will owe approximately $183,000 at the end of five years. If you purchased the home for $250,000 and it appreciates at 4% per year, it will be worth a little over $304,000 at that point. So the $50,000 you put into the home when you bought it, your down payment or equity, will now be worth over $120,000 (the value of the home $304,000 minus what you owe at $183,000). Does that make sense?"

"Yeah," Janis replied. "I'm following you."

"I know you don't like the thought of having debt, but let's talk for just a minute about a couple of the advantages of having a mortgage loan. The last three items on the list—the tax advantage, the forced savings, and the leveraged investment—are all related to your mortgage. Let's look at your situation specifically. According to your application, you are paying $1,000 per month for rent. If you purchased a home for $200,000 and borrowed $160,000 on a thirty-year fixed-rate loan at 6%, which is higher than current rates, your principal and interest payment would be $959. You'd pay over $9,500 in interest for a full year of payments. Let's also say that the property tax for the home is $2,000 per year. You can deduct both of those when tax time comes, meaning you can reduce your taxable income by $11,500 minus your standard deduction. If you are in a 25% tax bracket, you have reduced your annual tax bill by about $1,400 per year. So even if you are adding the taxes ($167 per month) and homeowner's insurance, guessing another $70 per month, the total payment on a house at this price is less than $100 more per month when you consider the tax savings.

"Having a loan provides somewhat of a forced savings, in that part of the monthly payment is going toward the balance of the loan. In the loan referenced above, there is only about $160 per month going to principal reduction over the first couple of years. But that is still money going in your pocket from an equity perspective. Your loan would be paid down from $160,000 to $153,800 after three years, so you will have saved $6,200 over that time period. If your home appreciates at a 3% annual clip, it will be worth $218,500 at the end of three years. So you have gained an additional $18,500 over that time period from an investment of $40,000, which was your down payment. That is a return of over 13% annualized return on your initial investment, which shows you how buying a home with a mortgage is a leveraged investment. Neither of these advantages exists for renting a home. So you can see that the financial advantage for buying a home extends even beyond the personal significance of owning a place of your own."

"That makes a lot of sense," Janis said after taking a deep breath. "I guess I've never really broken the numbers down the way you did. But you are also using some assumptions, like the home is going to appreciate at a 3% rate, and that might not be accurate."

"You are correct," Stan replied. "I'm also not considering the extra costs involved in owning a home. Things like lawn care and general maintenance would be your financial responsibility if you own a home. It's a little more difficult to put a price tag on those things as they vary. I guess you could also consider the fact that tax laws can change as well, which would skew my numbers. But the reality is that the only way to make future assumptions is by looking at past performance and the current rules in play. Over the long haul, homes have appreciated around a 3% annual clip, and the government has always provided some type of tax break for homeowners.

"Let me give you one more example based on the figures we just discussed. It may not be that realistic, but I think it will prove a point. Let's say you bought that $200,000 house and borrowed the $160,000 from our previous example. But let's say that it never went up in value, and you made payments every month for thirty years to pay off the loan you took out. Let's also assume that someone could rent the house for the $1,000 per month that you are currently paying in rent. And since we are assuming the value never changes, we'll also ignore additional expenses you may have for maintenance and improvement. In this case, you will have paid close to $345,000 over that period in principal and interest payments on the loan to go along with another $85,000 for taxes and insurance, again assuming that neither changed for the thirty years. So you'll have paid $430,000 over thirty years. If you continued to rent at $1,000 per month and the rent never went up, you would pay $360,000 in rental payments over the thirty years. So you will have spent an additional $70,000 owning versus renting over the thirty years. However, at the end of that period you have also paid off the $160,000 loan, so you are still ahead by $90,000 in total equity. Even in a scenario as crazy as this, where the rent never goes up, you get no tax benefit from owning, and your home value stays the same, you still come out ahead. And we are making this entire assumption on the fact that paying $1,000 per month gets you an equivalent home that $200,000 would buy you. I'm not sure how realistic that is either in our market. It could easily cost you more in rent."

"Wow," Janis exclaimed, "when you describe it like that, owning a home is somewhat of a no lose scenario. I'm still not sure I like the idea of taking on the responsibility. But maybe I should consider buying a condo where at least I don't have to deal with a yard and exterior maintenance. You've certainly shown me the financial advantage of owning."

"That sounds like a great plan," Stan responded. "Based on what I know about you from your credit and application, it definitely makes sense from a financial perspective for you to buy a home, particularly if you are planning on staying in this area for a while. But you have to get comfortable with the idea and remember the advantages that the mortgage debt can actually bring you versus considering it a detriment to your overall financial well-being. Keep me posted as you move forward with your thought process. I'm happy to help you with any questions you may have."

With that, she stood up and reached her hand out to shake Stan's hand. As we walked out, she asked me if I owned a home. I told her that I didn't at this point, but that I would love to. I didn't go into any details, just told her that she was in much better shape financially than I was. She said, "Well, good luck with that. Hopefully you have learned as much today as I did."

I just laughed and told her that I'd learned quite a bit in the past couple of weeks hanging out with Stan.

What I learned from our meeting with Janis:

1. *There are actually good reasons for people not to be homeowners.*
2. *There are great reasons why homeownership makes sense.*
3. *When used properly, mortgage debt can be a positive contribution to my overall financial well-being.*

7

DEALING WITH CREDIT ISSUES

I took off Friday afternoon from my job so I could sit in on two appointments Stan had lined up. The first was with a young man who was a close friend of Stan's and was in a situation that I would quickly learn resembled mine. Before Chris arrived, Stan gave me the background on Chris's situation. He explained their relationship so I felt like I already knew Chris and in some ways felt like his kinsman before he even arrived. Chris, now in his early thirties, was a former Sunday school student of Stan's who had the kind of personality that Stan said energized a room. Everyone who met him liked him. His college buddies always claimed, "The party didn't get started until Chris came through the door." His energetic personality also gave him the tendency to jump headfirst into things before thinking them through. That is how it went for him in relationships, investments, and occupational choices.

Stan had talked to Chris regularly over the years since Chris graduated from high school, following both his successes and his failures. Chris had been an average student at Middle Tennessee State University. He was a proponent of C's get degrees. He majored in good times and ultimately earned a business degree in business management, which Stan thought was comical. Stan said that Chris had too much trouble managing himself. How the heck was he ever going to manage others?

Chris started out his career after college with a local firm that managed about 150 hospitals across the Southeast. It didn't take long for Chris to realize that sitting behind a desk working 8:00 to 5:00 wasn't his cup of tea. So when he sat in on a seminar explaining how he could make big bucks with investment property, he quit his job and went into real estate. However, he didn't learn that while leverage allowed him to multiply his earnings, leverage adds a level of risk to the equation. So when the real estate market took a tumble, so did Chris's once thriving business.

Chris was not alone in missing the signs of what was about to happen in the real estate market, both locally and abroad. His fate was no kinder than that of thousands of others who lost their fortunes when the market turned. For Chris, it resulted in several odd jobs over the next few years, as well as a significant amount of debt piling up and a credit rating that had spiraled down like Space Mountain at Disney World. He had finally landed on his feet from an employment standpoint. His best friend's father had recognized Chris's potential early on and thought that if he could somehow rein him in a little, he would be a great asset to his company. So, he offered Chris a low-level starting position with the promise that if he did the job well, he would quickly move him into a more prominent role with the company.

I liked Chris the moment Stan introduced us. When Chris walked in, he gave Stan what I call a "man hug," the kind where you shake hands and hug at the same time. Chris really wanted two things from Stan. The first he made clear was Stan's advice on how to repair his credit so that he could buy a home. The second was much more subtle. I could tell from what Stan had told me, and how Chris was interacting with Stan, that he was looking for Stan's blessing. Chris had seen some pretty tough years, but he was finally getting back on top of things and he wanted Stan to recognize that. Stan had been a mentor to Chris, and it was easy to see in the way they communicated with each other that there was sort of a father to son or at least a big brother-little brother relationship between the two. I could tell that it was very important for Chris's self-confidence to hear Stan say that he still had confidence in Chris.

Josh had pulled Chris's credit report and given a copy to Stan minutes into the meeting. Stan was reviewing it as Chris sat anxiously. Stan looked up from the report and said, "Chris, I can tell you from my initial glance at your credit report that it's going to be tough for you to buy anything right now." Chris's credit score was lower than it would need to be, and the reason was primarily due to a large amount of credit card debt. There were also some older delinquencies that were not helping. Stan continued, "I'm sure there is some background explanation that you can share with us that will provide a little more detail to your situation. I already know that you can fix the situation if you set your mind to it. From high school on we've talked about the dangers of credit cards and how they seem to make your life easy, or even fun, but it's only for a time. You always pay the piper in the end. Guess what, it's time to pay the piper."

Chris loved Stan but was a little concerned by Stan's initial comments and wanted to make sure that Stan understood, so he interrupted. "You realize that all of those credit card debts occurred during the hard times I've had over the past few years. I paid off the judgment that was filed against me five or six years ago and the more recent collection as well. I never filed for bankruptcy when my attorney told me I should. Even though I didn't exactly follow your advice, I remember what you taught me about trying not to borrow money. So I know how important it was to pay people back when I did. I have paid back everyone that I owed anything to, and I'm working on getting on top of the credit cards. Doesn't that count for something?"

"Absolutely," Stan replied, "and I should not have started out the business part of our conversation on a negative note like that. Forgive me."

Chris gave Stan a thumbs-up, and Stan could tell that Chris's agitation was under control.

"You are right," Stan continued. "You have done an admirable job, in light of some pretty difficult circumstances, to keep your head above water and maintain your character throughout your struggle. I commend you for that. Many others, who did not have the same conviction as you, would have filed for bankruptcy and walked away from the situation and the people they owed. You also realize that you got yourself into this position, and now it's up to you to get out of it. That's really what I meant when I said, 'It's time to pay the piper.' You now have the resources to start digging your way out, and there is no better time to start than right now.

"Before we discuss your strategic approach, I want to make sure you understand what goes into determining your credit and what your credit score means. Other than your ability to repay, which is determined by looking at your overall employment and income picture compared to your monthly expenses, your credit rating is probably the next most important factor in determining your ability to qualify for a loan. It determines your willingness to pay as it provides a track record for how you have paid back money you have borrowed in the past. Theoretically, proof that you paid bills on time in the past is a solid indication that you will continue to do so. Granted, a credit report is black and white, while many times it should be in color. What I mean by that is that the credit report tells the results of the story but doesn't really tell the story itself. Take your credit report, for example. With the amount of credit card debt you have, it might be easy for one to assume that you just like to have a good time and spend too much money. Anyone who knows you personally might come to the same conclusion. However, you and I both know that you have been living life, at least over the past few years, very meagerly and that the debt was part of a business failure."

"Yeah," Chris admitted, "I probably did spend more than I should have back when things were going great, but these past four or five years have been nothing but peanut butter-and-jelly lunches to go with rice and beans for dinner!"

Stan had to chuckle, then continued, "When we pull a credit report, it is basically a compilation of information from all three credit bureaus, Trans Union, Equifax, and Experian. We call it a 'tri-merged' report because it compiles data from all three bureaus onto one report. Each bureau provides a representative score based on the data gathered. We'll talk more in just a minute about how each individual score is derived, but I want you to see the big picture at this point. Assuming we have a score from all three bureaus, we will use the middle score as your representative score for qualification purposes. Because not all data is reported to every bureau, using a middle score gives the fairest average. This is the number that we call 'your credit score.' The reason I said 'assuming' is that sometimes you don't have a score with a particular bureau. This could be because of inaccurate data or lack of data. In cases where you have less than three scores, we would use the lower of the scores available as your representative score. Does that make sense?"

Chris nodded, but asked, "What if two scores are the same? Oh, and what the heck is my score?"

"Good question," Stan replied. "In a situation where two of the scores are the same, the score that matches will likely become your middle score. In other words, if the two top scores are the same, one of the two becomes the middle score, and if the two bottom scores are the same, then one of those scores becomes the middle. So if your three scores are 734, 720, and 734 from the respective bureaus, your middle score would be 734. Also, if you do not have at least two valid scores due to lack of credit, we would have to do manual underwriting. In that case we can't get an automated approval through the underwriting system that we use. When that happens, we would have to get nontraditional credit to prove you have been making timely payments. We would use things like insurance, utility payments, phone bill, memberships to clubs, and anything where we could show a history of making twelve months of timely payments. Since you have legitimate scores, that is not necessary."

"I got it," Chris interjected, "but you are stalling. What is my score?" Chris knew from the "pay the piper" comment that it wasn't going to be great, and he could tell by the way Stan was explaining things that had little or no bearing on his specific scenario that he was putting off the inevitable.

"In your case," Stan said, "you have scores from each bureau so we have a valid score to use to qualify you for a loan. Your three scores are 623, 589, and 602. So the score that will be used for qualifying is 602 since that is the middle score. However, because all of the loan programs that we offer require a credit score of at least 620 or better, we are going to have a little bit of work to do before we will be able to qualify you for a loan. The good news is that you're not that far off, and I already see some areas where I think we can make progress toward improving your score. We will talk about that in just a minute. First, I want to make sure you understand what goes into making up the individual scores to begin with. It is important that you understand this as it will not only impact the significance of how you handle credit going forward but will also play a role in how quickly we can improve your current situation, so let's talk about how we can do that.

"The most important component of determining a credit score is how well payments have been made historically. Every creditor that you borrow money from will typically report your account and summary of payment history to the various credit bureaus. So, making your payments on time is critical to developing a solid credit rating. Not paying bills on time will have a negative impact on your credit and ultimately your score. Creditors report late payments in thirty-day increments of time. Typically, a delinquent payment will show up as a thirty-, sixty-, or ninety-day late payment. Obviously, the longer the payment is delinquent, the larger the negative impact on the score and rating. Many times, if the late payment extends beyond ninety days, the account can result in a collection or charge-off. This is when the creditor stops trying to collect on a bill and turns it over to another agency to try collecting from you or just writes the debt off as a loss. The creditors aren't really expecting to be paid in either scenario. They are happy when they do get paid and will reflect the collection or charge-off as paid. The delinquency doesn't go away, and these are even more significant than just being late on payments because they can hurt the rating even further. Many times when borrowers get in that type of position, where payments just can't be

made, it can ultimately lead to bankruptcy or foreclosure if they have a mortgage. Things like bankruptcy, foreclosure, tax liens, and judgments are all viewed
in the most negative manner from a credit perspective and are incredibly detrimental to a credit rating. In situations like those, qualifying for a mortgage loan
may be prevented for two to seven years, depending on the type of delinquency
and the type of loan being requested. The problem with late payments, related
to a credit score and attempting to improve the score, is that the only thing that
remedies late payments is time. In other words, time must pass, with a clean
payment history, before improvement can be seen in the rating when the late
payments exist. The length of time needed for the score to improve will depend
on the severity of the lateness and other factors such as the type of other credit,
the number of open accounts, the balances on those accounts, and the length of
time they've been open.

"Speaking of length of time, another key component of a credit rating is
how recent the activity is on your credit report. Recent activity carries more
weight than older activity. In other words, a late payment that occurred ten
months ago is going to have a much more significant impact than a late payment
that occurred three years ago. While an excellent payment history over the past
twenty-four months doesn't guarantee a stellar credit score, it is better to have
recent activity that is excellent combined with older late payments than it is to
have an excellent past credit history but recent trouble. The more recent the
negative issue, the bigger the impact will be on the score.

"In your case, most of the late payments you had—and there were none
more than thirty days other than the collection and judgment—occurred at
least three years ago or more. Fortunately for you, you have done a better than
average job of keeping your bills paid. Other than the small collection showing
up from the collection agency, which I know you resolved a little over a year
ago, your credit payment history is free of any significant late payments. Even
though your score is not great, had you been late on anything recently, it would
have been much worse.

"Another significant component of determining your credit score, and this
one probably impacts you in a significant way, is the type of credit you have as
well as the balances on that credit. It is tough to say what the ideal combination
of types of credit is from a scoring standpoint. Obviously paying all payments
on time is the most important thing. Coming up with the combination of the
type of debt is more complicated. I do know this: having revolving debt, which

is what credit card debt is, and sizable balances on that type of debt can drive your score down. The magic number seems to be around 50% of what is available on the card. When your balance is over 50% of the availability, it can hurt your score, particularly if multiple cards are in that condition. The same issue occurs if you only have one card, but it is in that same condition. If, for example, you have a credit card that has availability of $4,000, and you have a balance of $3,000 on that card, you are at 75% of the card's availability. Chris, you have multiple cards in that situation, so your score is being lowered quite a bit due to that."

"Okay, so what do I specifically need to do?" Chris asked.

"Well, for starters, we are going to make sure that you have a very workable budget," Stan replied. "You know I've always told you not to spend more than 80% of what you are bringing home each month."

"Yeah, didn't exactly live up to that standard, did I?" Chris said with a laugh.

"No, maybe not, but that's not the point. Today is always the best day to start anything positive. The pain you have been in is going to allow you to put massive amounts of personal energy into fixing this. That is the point. It is time to overhaul your financial life!" Stan said as he went into immediate coaching mode. "You have a solid income with your new job, and I assume you are still living in that dumpy little bachelor pad with pretty cheap monthly rent." Stan grinned as he winked at Chris.

"You bet," Chris replied, somewhat proud of the fact that he had not made matters worse after his business crashed by continuing to live downtown and fake that he was still making the big bucks.

"Good," Stan said with approval, "we should be able to do some quick damage to this heap of credit card debt. Keep in mind, these reports typically reflect about a month behind. Your credit report shows you have six credit cards that have balances on them. It looks like four of them are maxed out at $5,500, $4,000, $3,500, and the big one at $10,000. The other two are at $2,500 on a $3,500 card, and $1,500 on a $3,000 card. Sound correct?" It sounded much worse when Stan read it out loud to him.

"Unfortunately, you are correct," Chris answered as he slumped down in his chair. He looked over at me somewhat sheepishly and said, "Nothing like an audience for my trip to the woodshed."

I laughed and told him, "You are in good company! I've already had my trip to the same shed!"

"Well, it's time to get to work," Stan stated as he glanced at me and then back to Chris as he continued in coaching mode. "We only need to bring up your credit score by about 17 points to get you in a position where your credit score won't prevent you from qualifying. Honestly, that will be the easy part. I can run a simulator that our credit reporting agency uses that will give an estimate of how much your credit score will improve based on paying the credit card debt down or off. That will give us a very good estimate of where to expect your score to wind up.

"My guess is that by paying down each of these to a point that is less than 50% of availability, your score will easily improve by 50 or more points, maybe even more. As opposed to just doing the bare minimum of what is needed to get you qualified for a loan, I would rather see you have the discipline to wipe the slate clean of the credit card debt completely before moving forward with your home purchase. Or I would at least like to see you have a significant part of it completely paid off. Based on the income from your new job and your current expenses, you should easily be able to apply $2,500 per month to the debt.

"Once you start getting the debts paid down, your required minimum payments will drop as well, freeing up even more money to be applied to the principal balance of the remaining debt. If you will get real serious about this, I mean like eating a lot more peanut butter and jelly, you could have all of the credit cards wiped out in less than eighteen months, maybe twelve months if you get crazy with it. I know that seems like a while, but it will pass faster than you realize."

Feeling much more encouraged at this point, Chris said, "I've been through a personal hell for almost six years now. Another year to year and a half is nothing, particularly when I see a future that excludes peanut butter-and-jelly sandwiches!"

"Chris, I love your enthusiasm. I always have," Stan said. "It will take this same type of energy and passion to follow through with the next steps. Any time you want to make a change to a behavior pattern or habit, it takes this type of energy and requires a laser focus on the task at hand. As much as I'd like to send you out there to buy your first home this afternoon, there is work to be done before that. I want you to sit down tonight and put pencil to paper and see how quickly you can realistically get the credit card debt wiped out. Budget every penny you spend on a monthly basis. Free up every penny in your budget that is possible to target toward paying debt down. Figure out anything that you can sell or get rid of, and come up with any other income-producing activities you can think of that will help provide more money that can be applied to paying the debt down. I want you to email me the numbers and your plan tomorrow. I'll call you back to discuss it with you before the end of the week. And I suggest that you get an accountability partner. It will help you tremendously by having someone who can help hold your feet to the fire. Knowing you have to report your progress regularly to someone else will help you with the discipline to stay on track. I'm happy to be that person if you would like to check in with me once a week. Heck, Mike here might be a good one for you. He has a similar situation of his own, and maybe the two of you could motivate each other."

I nodded approvingly.

With that Chris gave Stan a big hug. Not like the half hug when the meeting started. This time it was a full-on bear hug. Chris wasn't small, and it caught Stan a little off guard. But Stan is a pretty big dude and returned the hug with equal vigor. As Chris left the office, Stan was visibly pumped about the change in Chris and was excited to play a positive role in helping him. This was one of the neatest exchanges I'd ever seen between two people. I already had huge admiration for Stan. But I didn't realize at the time that I was starting to develop a passion for the way he was helping others.

What I learned from our meeting with Chris:

1. *Paying debts during hard times requires character.*
2. *Having a good credit rating is critical in general, but particularly when buying a home.*
3. *How well I pay debts is the number one factor in determining my credit score.*
4. *The balance of my credit cards will impact my score.*
5. *Several factors go into making up a credit score, and that score is critical to getting a mortgage.*

8

First-Time Home Buyers and Qualifying Basics

AFTER returning a couple of calls and a handful of emails, Stan was ready for his next office visit. He gave me a quick review of their credit report and application that Josh had put together and shared a few details with me that Phil had given him. I could tell before Paul and Staci Johnson walked into his office that Stan was going to love working with them. They had been referred to Stan from Phil Hinson, one of Stan's best friends. From what Stan told me, Phil was one of the better Realtors in our community. Stan and Phil shared several commonalities, but they had one supreme bond: they both loved the Tennessee Volunteers! Stan had told me that probably 90% of their conversations revolved around how well the Vols were doing at whatever sport was currently in season. Honestly, it was always football season: pre-season practice, the game of the week, bowl preparation, recruiting, signing day, spring drills, summer workouts, then back to pre-season practice. In addition to the Vols, Stan and Phil shared a love of real estate and, more important, a love of seeing home buyers have their dreams come true.

When they sat down in Stan's office, Paul gave Stan some quick background information. Paul met Staci in his last year at Union University in Jackson, Tennessee, when Staci was just a freshman. Staci had since graduated, and the two had been married for a year. Both sets of their parents had advised them that buying a home would be more financially beneficial for them than renting. Neither had high-paying jobs yet, and each had more student loans than they would have liked. On top of the significant student loan payments, they had a couple of car loans. On the positive side, they had done a great job saving up money for the down payment to buy a house. They had also done a great job of not carrying credit card debt. Paul's dad had instructed him specifically when he was a young man that credit card debt was evil and that he better never have any. So they had stopped by to discuss their situation with Stan and have him help them determine what made sense from an overall budgeting standpoint and how qualifying for a mortgage loan worked. They wanted to know if buying a home made sense right now, and if not, what things they needed to do to strategically help them be in a better position to buy a home as soon as possible.

Paul was the financial brains in the couple, and both were quick to admit that. Paul was a young sales executive for Genesco, Inc., a specialty retailer of branded footwear, headquartered in Nashville. Staci was a first grade schoolteacher for a small private school in East Nashville. Upon introduction, Paul described his business background and how he was just more naturally acclimated to numbers.

Staci admitted, "Yeah, I'm more left brained and struggle to understand financial concepts. My dad was an accountant so he always took care of our family's finances. So I'm thrilled to have Paul handle that for us."

"That's okay. I hope to make this simple enough for you to understand," Stan told Staci. "It is very important that you both have a solid understanding of the financial concepts we are going to discuss today. It's important that you leave here with your questions answered and with a solid comprehension of some basic financial concepts I want to share with you. I'm going to go over the basics about how you qualify for a mortgage loan, so I'm confident you will have a great grasp of that part before leaving. But more important, I hope to give you some strategies that will allow you to obtain a mortgage in a manner that strategically fits into a well-rounded overall financial strategy. Most people can ultimately qualify for a mortgage loan, but very few actually structure that loan so that it fits into an overall strategy designed to bring you financial success. I hope when you leave here today that both of you will have a clear understanding of how that works."

Stan could tell that Paul was very no-nonsense and wanted to get right down to the nuts and bolts of how the process worked to find out how much of a loan that he and Staci qualified for. Stan knew he was going to have to keep things more analytical to keep Paul engaged, while at the same time making sure he did not lose Staci. He asked them, "Tell me something before we dig into any numbers. What is the most important thing to each of you about buying a home?"

Paul spoke first, and he answered very much as Stan had anticipated. "We are tired of wasting our money paying rent, and we want our monthly payment to go toward an asset that will grow over time. I ran the numbers and figured that we lost about $5,000 in tax savings and potential appreciation last year alone. We are not too upset about it since we really didn't have any money to make a down payment after we got married, but I think we have enough now, so we want to make this happen."

When Staci got her turn, she responded in a manner that Stan expected. From the first ten minutes of conversation, Stan could tell that Staci was the nurturing type, who would ultimately desire security first and foremost when making decisions. She said simply, "I want a home where I can put down roots and raise my family."

"Those are great answers," Stan confirmed, "and I hope you see the significant difference between the two. Both of you have the same desire, to own a home, but clearly have very differing perspectives on what is important to you. I bring this up because it is crucial that you each have a clear view of the other's perspective on what is important. That actually applies to most things in life but is particularly important regarding the home-buying process."

Stan got really serious for a moment before continuing: "This is my opinion, and while your mortgage certainly fits in this category, what I'm about to tell you deals with a lot more than just the mortgage. It is very important that the two of you share in the overall management of your family's finances. I've seen way too many situations where one spouse controlled all the money issues. It's normally the man in the scenario, but I've seen it be the wife as well. There are just too many issues that can come up that will leave one of the partners in a painful position when both aren't active in handling the finances. Financial issues are probably the number one factor in marriages breaking down. As long as you approach your financial responsibilities as a partnership, where neither is left in the dark on anything, it will prevent any money issue from coming between the two of you." He could sense there was some uneasiness in the room, but based on his interpretation of the situation, Stan felt it was critical that they hear this.

"Understanding that the two of you see things a little differently, I want to ask one more question. What is the most important thing to you as it relates to borrowing money to buy a home?"

Again, Paul charged forward and said, "It's very important that we maximize what we can qualify for so we can buy something that we can grow into. Our income is going to continue to increase over the next several years, so it is important for me to be able buy as much home as possible now, even if the payments are a little more difficult for us right now."

Stan glanced over at Staci to see if she had another opinion to add.

"Well, I guess I agree," Staci said. "I'd love to buy a home now that we can raise our children in and not have to worry about buying again once our family starts to expand. I'd also like to keep the payment manageable so that we have some flexibility down the road if our income situation changes. I love working with children, but I also became a teacher so that my schedule would be flexible to some degree and would put me on the same routine as our children."

"Okay, that is great to know," Stan said. "That will help as we talk through the qualifying numbers and enables me to better understand the motivation behind your thought processes. We are going to discuss qualifying and how the numbers work, but I want to share a simple concept with you first. Will that be okay?"

Stan continued, "It doesn't necessarily fit within the framework of the numbers that we look at from a qualifying standpoint, but it is very important in establishing a complete financial plan. I've found that people fail financially for two reasons. They overextend, spending more than they should, or they don't have enough money saved to handle emergencies. Most of the time, the two things go hand in hand. Regardless of qualifying ratios, which we will discuss in a moment, I recommend that you establish a budget that will pay all of your monthly expenses with 80% of your net income. Keeping your monthly expenses within 80% of your budget will prevent you from overspending, and it frees up enough room to establish an appropriate savings fund. And as a long-term goal, I'd suggest that you put a plan in place to pay your mortgage balance down to 80% of the home's value. That is something to address once you have paid all of your other debts off, but it needs to be in the long-term plan. These are things we can discuss further in the future, but it is good to at least have the thought process on the front end."

When he finished his point, Stan sensed that Paul was a little perplexed, so he asked him "Paul, are you tracking with me?"

Paul said, "I'm completely in agreement with you on setting up the budget the way you describe. Never really heard it broken down that way before, but it makes complete sense. We have certainly done that up to this point, even though we weren't necessarily focused on a specific ratio. I still think it is important that we try to qualify for the maximum amount that we can get, but I certainly understand the issue of not overspending and needing to have money saved. I guess I'm still contemplating the suggestion you made about both of us getting involved in the overall financial process. Staci has never seemed to have any desire to be involved, so I've just kind of taken the bull by the horns and done it all. I guess I need to figure out how to get her engaged in that part of our partnership."

Even though he did not let it show, Stan was quite stunned at Paul's response but incredibly pleased at this reaction. Stan smiled and said, "That's the fun part of marriage, figuring out how to engage each other in the important things. That is also the difference between a successful partnership and one that fails. I know you two will figure it out. Now let's talk about buying a home!"

Everyone seemed to take a collective breath, and much of the heaviness that seemed to be in the room lifted. "I don't want you to stray too far from what I suggested about keeping your expenses at or below 80% of your income. I also feel it is very important to completely understand what a lender is going to be looking at related to your ability to qualify," Stan explained. "Also, please understand that initially, I will be speaking here in general terms as we address each topic. Every borrower's situation is different and has unique considerations.

"There are basically four components to qualifying for a mortgage, or what some may term your 'ability to repay.' Those components are your income, your credit, your cash needed to close, and your debt to income ratios. All have to be in order to qualify. My assistant, Josh, has put your application together and pulled credit, so we will look at your specific situation as it relates to each of these qualifying components. Does that sound like an acceptable plan?"

They agreed, so Stan began. "The ability to repay starts with establishing the income that will be used to repay the loan. Income, along with your credit rating, is probably the most important piece of the overall qualification. If you do not have adequate income to repay a loan, you will likely not qualify. Your specific situation is excellent from an employment standpoint. Paul, you have been with Genesco for the past 2.5 years, so you have great stability. Staci, even though you've only been with the school for just under a year, you started soon after graduation as well. We consider the time in school to count as employment when you are a full-time student, earning a degree that accompanies your current employment."

"Yep, I received my degree in education with a specialty in child psychology," Staci said.

"Excellent," Stan responded, "you guys should be in great shape from that standpoint then. Let's take a look at some income numbers as we work toward what you can qualify for. Staci, we'll start with yours since it is straightforward. Since your pay is all base salary, we'll just take your annual salary of $36,000 and divide it by twelve. So there will be $3,000 per month of income to use when qualifying you. Paul, since you have both a salary and a commission component of your pay, we are going to have to look a little more closely at determining the income that we can use as your qualifying amount. While salary is taken at face value, commission income has to be averaged over a two-year period.

"In your situation, Paul, we can count your salary at face value. Since your base is $18,000 per year, we can simply divide $18,000 by twelve to determine that $1,500 per month is what we can count from a qualifying standpoint related to the base salary."

Paul spoke up somewhat disagreeably, "But I make a lot more than that!"

Stan raised his hands as if to say "calm down" and said, "I completely understand that your pay structure is designed for the majority of your income to be earned via your sales efforts and is paid to you in the form of commission. I also see based on the tax forms you have provided, as well as your year-to-date pay stub, that you are doing very well and improving consistently. That is very important from the eyes of an underwriter and will be reviewed in a positive light – much better than if the situation were the opposite, where your income might have declined year over year. However, it is also critical that you under-stand we can't qualify you based on the total of what you are making right now since the commission income has to be averaged. Because commission income is variable, we look at the history of the income to determine what can be used to qualify versus what you are making right now. Since we are still early in the year, it is very likely that an underwriter will average your last two years plus year-to-date commission to determine the figure we can use for qualification. Based on my calculations, your commissions should average out to a total of $2,500 per month. When we add that to your base salary of $1,500 per month, we have $4,000 per month that we can use for qualifying you."

Stan could easily see the disappointment on Paul's face. Paul shook his head and actually said, "That's disappointing. It would seem that since my income is increasing, as you pointed out, we should at least be able to use what I've made this year and average it out with just last year."

"While I don't completely disagree with you," Stan countered, "the best way to estimate future commission earnings is to average those prior earnings. Fourteen months is likely too short a time period to go on when determining variable income. The good news is that you have not any non-reimbursed business expenses. So we will be able to use the average of the written off totals without deducting anything."

Paul came back with, "Yeah, the one thing my employer does to offset the pretty meager salary they pay me is to pay all my expenses. The reality is that it is a great job, and I enjoy what I do. If I can stay on pace, it should be financially rewarding for us in the not too distant future."

Stan nodded and smiled, "Truth is, you are doing pretty doggone good right now. I don't know too many other twenty-six-year-olds out there who are on pace to make $60,000 plus this year!" Paul eased back into his chair and Stan continued with the next qualifying component.

"Because one of the main considerations in determining ability to repay is making sure that there is enough income to pay monthly expenses, we will also consider the relationship between your income and debt obligations. We call this your debt to income ratio. Generally, your monthly mortgage payment, insurance, property taxes, and any association-type dues should not be more than about 30% of your gross monthly income. That simply means that you divide your total housing payment by your gross monthly income, and the percentage should not exceed 30%.

"My recommendation is that your total payment ratio, which includes all monthly debt obligations including new housing payment, generally be under 40%. Simply add your monthly housing payment to all other monthly debt payments like car or installment loans, credit cards and the like, and divide by your gross monthly income. That figure needs to be less than 40%. You don't have to count groceries, gas, cable, and those kinds of payments, however. Although this is not an absolute rule, and will vary dependent on all the other factors, like credit score and down payment amount, it is a good rule of thumb. Most loan programs will allow a total debt ratio of 45% with good credit, so there is some flexibility in my suggestion to keep the total debt ratio at or below 40%.

"And please don't forget what I mentioned about keeping your expense at or below 80% of your net income. We'll want to use that as an overriding guide. It is very evident by the savings you have been able to accumulate over the past year that you are supersavers. I just want to make sure that you continue on that path. The only way to do that is to make sure that your monthly expenses, of which your house is a big part, stay within that manageable number that allows you to keep saving going forward. Your house payment plus all other expenses needs to stay at or below 80% of your monthly net income.

"Now let's take a look at your debts. According to your credit report, you have a car loan that is $550 per month, another car loan at $350 per month, and student loans totaling $335 per month for a total of $1,235 per month. You've done a great job by not adding any additional credit card debt. We've already determined your monthly qualifying income to be $7,000 per month. If we use the 45% number for your total debt ratio, then you have $3,150. This is what you can use for total debt payments. Subtracting the $1,235 for other obligations leaves you $1,915 to use for a house payment. Normally I think getting to 45% is pushing the envelope and can be a little dangerous from an overall budget perspective, particularly if that kind of debt obligation makes additional savings difficult. That is why I normally use 40% as my general rule. However, in your case, I'd suggest that this is fine since your income is actually more than what we are able to use to qualify you."

Paul seemed more comforted after hearing that he could qualify for a payment of up to $1,900. He told Stan, "I think Phil should be able to find us a home in the area of town where we want to buy and keep the payment in that range. I'd like a little more flexibility, but we should be able to make that work."

Encouraged by this, Stan moved ahead. "Before we talk about down payment and cash to close for your specific scenario, I do want us to review a couple of things that are relevant to your payment and budgeting. Now that we know what the qualifying payment can be, let's make sure that having a payment at that level will still be manageable.

"Your scenario is a little bit different because your income fluctuates and is really more on a monthly basis than what we are using from a qualifying standpoint. So we have to take that into consideration when establishing the parameters for the 80% budget. If we split the difference between what Paul made last year and has made year to date, your monthly income comes to about $7,400 per month. If you bring 75% of that home after taxes, that is $5,500 per month net. So to stay within 80% of that figure, you'd need to be at $4,500 per month in expenses. If you buy a house with a $1,900 payment and have $1,300 in monthly debt payments already committed, that leaves you $1,200 for the remainder of your monthly expenses if you are going to be able to save and give the first 20% that you make. I just want to make sure you are tracking with me on this."

"Yeah, I think we are well within that number," Paul said confidently and pointed out, "No way we'd be able to save what we saved last year if we weren't tracking on that one."

"I couldn't agree more," Stan said as he nodded. "Just wanting to make sure you stay on that path. Once you buy the home, it gets easy to let expenses get away from you, doing things like furnishing the home and paying for things that you need to work on the home. Before you realize it, you have completely gotten out of the habit of giving and saving, and every penny is getting spent on expenses. Just remember how easily that can happen, and avoid the temptation of having everything you want in the home immediately.

"Let's talk a little more specifically now about the up-front money needed to buy a home. Keep in mind that ultimately, I want to help you get to where your mortgage is 80% or less of the value of your home. Historically, 20% of the value of the home has been the standard down payment. However, many loan types require less than that, and we'll discuss those. If you are putting down less than 20%, as your lender, we will scrutinize your loan more from an underwriting standpoint since you are more of a risk from our standpoint. We will also require private mortgage insurance, which in our business is referred to as PMI or simply MI. That helps protect the lender against default. Depending on the type of loan and percentage of down payment, the cost of the mortgage insurance on a monthly basis can vary. But the payment can be pretty significant. As an example, on an FHA loan with minimum down payment (3.5%) on a $250,000 sales price, the monthly mortgage insurance payment will be over $250 per month.

"If you are able to put at least 5% down, then you will likely consider a conventional loan, which will have a smaller mortgage insurance payment assuming you have good credit. This is likely what I'll recommend to you guys," Stan smiled at them and said, "because your credit is excellent and according to your application, looks like you have enough to invest the 5%."

Stan pulled out their credit report from his file and laid it on the table in front of them. He showed them that Paul's three scores were 775, 782, and 790, so his middle score, the one that would be used for qualifying, was 782. Staci's scores were 790, 797, and 802, so her qualifying score was 797. At this, Staci stood up and let out a "Ha! My score is better than yours!"

Paul could only shake his head. He looked up at Stan and asked how this was possible.

Stan replied, "While I love the competitiveness, the truth is that both of these scores are phenomenal! You will receive the best rate and fee scenario with those scores. My guess is that Staci's is a little better because she has a couple of accounts that have been open a little longer than yours."

"Well, that's only because her parents signed on a couple of cards for her in college!" Paul retorted.

Grinning ear to ear, Staci exclaimed, "Whatever it takes, baby!"

"There is something important that I need to point out here," Stan said, still tickled at Staci's behavior. "You have been given a good example that you should follow when you have children of your own. It makes great sense, if done using the proper amount of discernment, to help your children as they get late in the high school days or early in college to start establishing credit. I'm not suggesting that you turn them loose with a credit card or borrow for school or a car, but putting a credit card in their name, with you as the co-signer and ultimate over-seer, can get them in a much better position from a credit rating standpoint than making them wait until they have graduated from college and have a job to be able to start establishing it on their own.

"There is one last thing I'll recommend to you, and Phil can help you with this. You might consider asking the seller to pay some or all of your closing costs for you. Paying your closing costs and prepaid items, which are basically the interest and costs to set up an escrow account for taxes and homeowner's insur-ance, can run anywhere between 1.5% and 4% of your sales price, depending on the amount.

"Most loans will allow a certain percentage to be paid by the seller on your behalf. Granted, the seller will likely build in the cost of whatever he or she is paying on your behalf into the price of the home. In other words, if a seller is asking $200,000, but willing to take $195,000, you can either offer $195,000, paying your own costs, or offer $200,000 asking the seller to pay $5,000 of your costs. Either offer is the same since the seller will net $195,000 both ways. Keep in mind the house has to appraise for the price you offer. But again, this is where Phil will help you make the best decision."

As Stan put all of their documents back into his file, he finished with this: "There are other things I want us to talk about further. So I suggest that once you have been out with Phil and have a good idea of the price home you might be interested in purchasing, we visit again either here or on the phone. We'll need to discuss loan types. With everything else we discussed today, we did not discuss the difference between a fixed rate and an adjustable rate loan. There are some hybrid-type loans, where the rate is fixed for five, seven, or even ten years, before moving to an adjustable phase, that we will want to consider. It will depend on the home you are looking at and the timeframe you think you will be living there. Since most first-time home buyers don't stay in a home more than seven years, it is certainly something we want to look at.

"I also want to look at a plan for getting those cars and student loans paid off sooner than later. And finally, we need to set up a plan for getting your loan balance paid down to 80% of the home's value as soon as we can. All of that would probably be a little overwhelming considering everything that we went over today, but each concept I mention now plays a key role in establishing a foolproof financial strategy."

"That sounds like a great plan," Paul responded. "A friend of mine just bought a new home, and they did a seven-year ARM, so I'm a little familiar with that program and agree that it is something that might benefit us. We'll definitely want to discuss that further. I really appreciate the detail you went into today to make sure we understand the qualifying process. I am even more appreciative that you took time to share with us your thoughts on how we can map out an overall financial strategy. We are definitely going to spend some time reviewing the concepts that you have given us today. And we are going to do all of it together as a team."

With that, Stan shook their hands, and we walked out with them. Stan wanted some water, and I needed some coffee.

What I learned from our meeting with Paul and Staci:

1. *For those who are married, finances should be handled as a team where both understand the money flow and both are involved in all significant financial decisions.*
2. *There are four basic components to qualifying for a mortgage loan - employment/ income; credit; assets/cash to close; and debt ratios.*
3. *Income earned from employment is the source of repaying a loan so is probably the most significant measure of someone's ability to qualify.*
4. *The down payment will determine the type of loan needed, and money for closing must be properly documented and come from an acceptable source.*

5. *Debt ratios protect borrowers from overextending.*

6. *The type of debt I have and how well I pay my payments will determine my credit score – which impacts not only my qualifying, but also my terms of payment.*

7. *When buying a home, always consider what the future looks like, particularly potential employment changes and future expenses that don't exist now.*

8. *Contracts are negotiable – if it makes sense, I can ask the seller to help pay some of my costs if needed.*

9. *When I have kids one day, I should help them establish credit in a responsible way.*

More on Qualifying, Mortgage insurance, and Using a Realtor

S TAN texted me over the weekend and asked if I could come to his office on Monday. But instead of coming early, he wanted me to come at 6:30 p.m. I got no other details. When I walked into Stan's office, Josh was setting up a camera on Stan's computer and had the dial up ready to go for a video conference. Stan was pretty old school and was accustomed to doing most of his initial interviews with clients face-to-face or just over the phone, so this was a little out of the ordinary. I found out later that this was only the second time Stan had done an initial application interview via a video conference. I'm not so sure if I was invited for my benefit or for Stan's. Josh was going home as soon as the conference started, and I think Stan liked the idea of having me there in case something went wrong with the technology.

Juan and Benita Santiago had worked with a financial planner in Alabama who was good friends with a local financial planner and one of Stan's buddies. When his buddy called to introduce the Santiagos to Stan the week before, Stan was in the car and had pulled off to the side of the road to take basic notes on a notepad he always kept in his console. The basic gist that Stan got was that Dr. Santiago had lost a bunch of money in a bad business move, had gotten a new job in Nashville that started in a month, had his current home to sell in Alabama, and wanted to know if he could buy a house when he moved up here.

Apparently there had been a time when Dr. Santiago's medical practice was thriving. But a couple of bad investments and a significant turn for the worse in the economy had left him and Mrs. Santiago sideways on their mortgage and seeking a new start. They were huge University of Alabama football fans and came to Nashville whenever their beloved Crimson Tide played Vanderbilt. From their travels to Middle Tennessee, they decided that the Nashville area would be a great place to live.

When Dr. Santiago got a call from a clinic in town that specialized in pediatric foot care, they decided to move north to Tennessee. Now they needed help getting a new home. Dr. Santiago assured Stan that he would go into much more detail when they did their conference call, but what he mainly wanted to know was whether they qualified for a loan to buy a home based on the new job, and if so, did they need to sell their current home to qualify. That was really all they discussed other than the upcoming SEC football season.

The reason Dr. Santiago couldn't discuss all the details the week before was because he insisted "that my wife be engaged in the process – I never have any conversations on something this big that will impact both of us unless she is completely involved." So even though Stan did not know as much as he normally would at this point in a conversation with the client, he knew that he already liked how the Santiagos operated. Even if their financial situation was a mess, he knew that the Santiagos were handling things as a team, and there would be no need for counseling on that end. Stan could tell that was important to Dr. Santiago, so he was certainly willing to accommodate the request.

When we got the Santiagos on the video conference, Mrs. Santiago began the conversation and led off with the story of where they had come from. "Stan, to tell you these last few years have been challenging would be an understatement." She was fighting back tears as she continued. "I thought that once we got the kids out of the house, things would get much easier, at least from a financial standpoint. I guessed wrong on that one. And please don't misunderstand and think that I'm pointing my finger at Juan. I'm just as guilty with our financial difficulties as he is. We have always approached everything as a team. I was 100% in favor of Juan expanding his practice when he did. There is no way that we saw a combination of both the economy turning the way it did and the insurance companies that support our client base changing their policies related to pediatric foot care, all at the same time."

She added, "We thought we were making a business move that would provide us enough income over the next seven to eight years that would allow us to easily retire at whatever point we wanted to after that. And truthfully we probably held on too long once we realized we had added too much space to our office, but at that point, it was too late to do much other than what we did.

By the time we sold Juan's practice, it took everything we had in our savings to pay back the loan that we had taken out for the expansion. So here we are close to the end of our working life, in a time period that we thought we'd be riding off into the sunset, starting over again. And with everything we've been through here, we just want to start over and do it in a new place. Our three children have moved away. Truthfully a move to the Nashville area would get us closer to them, and we really love the area. So we need your help as we hope to make this final journey."

Stan responded to Benita with poignant grace, thanking her for being so transparent about her situation. "Benita, it is great to know the story behind the story as it helps me better understand why you want to buy a home. And let me tell you first and foremost how much I admire you for your commitment to pay back borrowed money. I can't tell you how many times I've seen people encounter similar situations to yours and walk away from everything. It would have been much easier for you and Dr. Santiago to have walked away from your obligation to the bank and protected your savings. It was an incredibly honorable thing to do, and I greatly respect your decision."

"It was really not a thought for us," Benita replied. "We made the decision knowing that if it did not work out, we would be responsible for any money borrowed. We knew we were not borrowing more than what we had in our savings. If the very worst thing happened, we'd be able to pay off what we owed and protect our credit. We really thought we were making a wise investment, but we decided on the front end that we'd deal with any costs of our failure."

Stan said, "That is very admirable, and the fact that you protected your credit will help with your next venture."

Dr. Santiago spoke up at this point. "We are confident that our credit is good. But we did not want anyone pulling our credit report until we had a good idea of whether this will work. Obviously we don't have much money left now in our savings account, and we took out a second mortgage on our house to help with the business, so we won't have very much if anything coming out of the sale of the home. Fortunately, we don't have any other debt, and we were able to manage to hold onto about $25,000 in our savings that will be available to buy something there. But my pay will be a lot lower there than it has traditionally been here. I've agreed to take a starting salary of $150,000 with the practice where I will be working in Nashville."

He continued, "We have no intention of keeping our house here, but we have not put it on the market to sell it yet either. So we need to know what we can afford there and if there is a possibility to buy something with what we have available without selling our home here. We have done some preliminary figures and realize that it will be very tight. So we would not only like to know what can and can't be done. We would like your counsel as well. We have not bought a home in more than twenty years, but I'm hoping that a lot of this will be like riding a bike, and it will come back to us as we experience it. Right now, it feels like it's our first time. You come very highly recommended, so we'd love your thoughts."

"Well, I think I can help you with that," Stan responded. "If we can't help you with what you want right now, I am certain that we can put together a good plan for you. I'm not going to go into a lot of specifics yet, but I want you to know that there are basically four components to qualifying for a home loan. Your employment and income combine for the first major component, your credit is the second, confirming cash to close is third, and the final one is making sure your debt ratios are in line.

"Since you are moving from a self-employed situation to a salaried position, we will be able to give you full credit for the income that you will be earning in your new position. If you had been moving from a salaried position to a self-employed position, it would have been dramatically different. You would have likely had to wait for at least two years before you would have been able to qualify for a loan. We will ultimately have to check your credit. This will require pulling a credit report to determine that you are in good shape from an overall credit standpoint and get confirmation of your credit score. For now, we will assume, based on what you have told me, that the credit is excellent. Assuming that you can put down at least 5%, you will likely be looking at a conventional loan. Both your interest rate and the cost of the mortgage insurance, which you will be required to pay since you are putting less than 20% down, depend on your credit score when doing a conventional loan.

"The fourth and final piece to qualifying will be your debt to income ratios. This is a simple calculation we do to determine the amount of monthly payments you have for all of your debt as a percentage of the new income you will be earning here. This is going to be the key calculation in your situation that will determine your ability to purchase here without selling your home there, so we are going to spend most of our time on this part of the qualification. Let me ask you a couple of questions. How much are you paying currently for your house, including taxes, insurance, and the second mortgage? Also, I know you have spent some time here in Nashville when the Tide rolls into town to play Vandy. Have you given some consideration to where you want to live and what kind of price range you are looking to buy?"

Dr. Santiago replied, "We have really visited only the areas right around Vanderbilt. But that is pretty close to where I'll be working, so we are okay with that area. We hope to find a home without needing a Realtor and save as much as possible. Benita has found a couple of nice homes already. Most are in the $400,000 to $450,000 range. Our total payment on the home in Alabama is right at $2,600. Honestly, we'd like to keep the payment on the home in Nashville in that same range. Based on our expected budget there, the payment needs to be in that range for us to manage our finances in the manner that we want."

"Okay, that helps a lot and gives us the figures we need to determine whether this will work. Remind me to discuss some thoughts on getting help finding a home before we finish, but first, let's discuss your financial situation. Since you only have $25,000 to work with on this deal, you will likely only have enough money to put down 5% on the type of price range you are looking at. Only conventional loans and FHA loans will allow you to put that little down. Because your credit score is so good, it is going to make more sense for you to go with a conventional loan. I'll explain that better in just a minute. But the main point here is that both of these two loan types have a limit on the amount available.

"The conventional loan limit in our area is $417,000. So you are going to be limited to a sales price of about $440,000. At that price, you will have to put down $23,000 to keep your loan amount in the conventional price range. If you go over that loan amount, you would be looking at getting a jumbo loan – which is a loan amount over the conventional loan limit. Most jumbo loans require more down payment than 5%, so are not likely options. Keep that in mind as you consider the price range.

"If you buy a home priced at $440,000, you would be looking at a total payment of about $2,900. At a loan amount of $417,000, your payment for principal and interest will be $2,238 at 5% interest on a thirty-year fixed-rate loan. I'm assuming homeowner's insurance will be $1,500 per year and taxes around $4,200 per year. That comes out to $475 per month when annualized. Mortgage insurance, which we will review in just a moment, will be about $187 per month. That all adds up to a payment of $2,900 per month. Add the $2,900 to the $2,600 that you are paying for the current home and you have a total monthly expense of $5,500. We take that total and divide that by the amount of your monthly income.

"Since your new salary will be $150,000, that is a monthly total of $12,500. Dividing the payments by this amount gives us a total of 44%. You are allowed to have a qualifying ratio of up to 45% on a conventional loan that is structured this way. So assuming that there are no other debts and that your credit is excellent like your assumption, you should qualify from a ratio perspective."

"Oh, you don't know how happy that makes us!" Benita interjected. "With everything that we have been through, the ability to move forward without needing to sell our home here first would be so helpful."

Stan warned, "As you can see, you are very tight on this part of the qualifying. So we need to move forward very cautiously, and you need to go ahead and run the numbers to make sure that you are okay from a budgeting standpoint. Carrying two mortgage payments for any extended period of time can be quite a burden, so I just want to make sure that you are comfortable with that before you go down that road. I know that you don't intend for that situation to last for a long time, but you need to be prepared for all circumstances, particularly if you are tight on what the home will sell for versus what you owe, and know that you will have to sell at a specific price point to at least break even on the sale."

Dr. Santiago replied, "Yes, Benita and I will need to have further discussions on this matter, but it is nice to know that the option is there if we decide to proceed in that manner. Now, can you give us some more detail about the mortgage insurance?"

"That is actually a great transition," Stan declared. "As I mentioned, mortgage insurance is required when you are borrowing more than 80% of the sales price. This insurance is for the lender. It is protection against potential default from the borrower. So while you are required to pay for it, it really doesn't provide any protection for you – it is for your lender. It is a necessary evil that gives people, who are in situations like yours, the ability to get financing without having to come up with a 20% down payment. Let's use the example we were discussing earlier and assume you buy a home for $440,000, putting 5% down and borrowing $417,000. If you were to default on the loan two years into the payments, when you had paid the balance down to say $405,000, and the home had to be sold in the market as a distress sale, where the lender was able to recoup $375,000, the mortgage insurance would kick in at that point and pay the lender the $30,000 shortage on what was still owed on the loan. Does that make sense?"

They both simultaneously answered, "It does."

"Good," Stan said. "There are a couple of other important factors to understand about mortgage insurance. First, the cost of the mortgage insurance obviously depends on the amount you borrow, but it also depends on your credit score. The better your score, the more likely you are to get the cheapest rate. From that standpoint, mortgage insurance resembles regular insurance where the cheapest rates go to the least risky customers. The second issue is that there are actually a couple of ways to pay for it. The most common way is to pay the monthly amount required. But you can also pay it in lump sum at closing, or you can roll the cost back into the financing of the home by your willingness to take a higher rate on the mortgage versus paying a monthly payment. Doing it this way will typically result in a lower payment. For example, if you borrow using the scenario we described where you borrow $417,000 at 5%, your payment with mortgage insurance is $2,426, not counting taxes and insurance. If you were able to finance the mortgage insurance by taking a rate of 5.5% on the loan, the principal and interest payment would be $2,367 or $59 per month cheaper than paying the monthly mortgage insurance. However, if you go that route, the payment is permanently set at the higher rate. One advantage of paying the mortgage insurance on a monthly basis is that you have the ability to drop the mortgage insurance once you have the loan paid down to 80% of the home's value at the time. You almost always have to pay the mortgage insurance for at least two years regardless of your equity position. But In a typical appreciation environment, you are likely to get the loan paid down to the 80% level in four to five years. You have to do an appraisal at the time to confirm the value. But once you are to that point, you can remove the MI permanently. So at that point, the payment would be about $130 cheaper than the payment would have been taking the higher rate and avoiding the monthly mortgage insurance. So the decision ultimately comes down to how long you think you will be living in the house and paying on that specific loan."

Stan went on, "Remember that the loan can always be refinanced and the loan to value on the refinanced loan will be based on the current appraised value. But with rates as low as they are right now, refinancing may not ever be a really attractive option as you wouldn't want to refinance if the rate were higher than where you are now. I hope this makes sense to you, but know that you don't have to make any decisions about this right now. It will be easier to decide the best course of action once you have a home picked out and have a better idea for not only the specific payments on it, but also how long you think you will want to live there."

"That makes a lot of sense, and we appreciate you going into detail to describe it for us," Dr. Santiago said.

"You are welcome," Stan replied. "There are a couple of other things that I want us to discuss in more detail at some point in the future that we will put on the shelf for now. Once you get your plan in place for moving, I want you to be thinking long term about building your savings back up to a position to serve you well in case of an unexpected need. I would also love to see you have a plan in place to get your mortgage paid down to 80% of the home's value. If you go the route where you are paying mortgage insurance on a monthly basis, I want you to work on getting to a point where you can get that removed. Once you sell your home in Alabama, you will free up a lot of room in your monthly budget to apply to both of these things. I know that getting moved and getting settled here are the priority right now, but it doesn't hurt to have these thoughts in the background because they are critical to obtaining the best overall financial position for your family."

"Stan, I can't begin to tell you how much we appreciate the time you have given us today," said Dr. Santiago. "You have made us feel better about our situation now and about where we are headed. We are so excited about this next chapter of our lives, and we are very grateful to have someone like you on our side. Speaking of having someone on our side, you asked me to remind you about discussing the thought process of doing this without a Realtor. Our thought was that even if there is a listing agent, like the one we are using to sell our house, we figured we could get a cheaper price on the one we are buying by not having someone represent us when we purchased a home there."

"I certainly won't argue that there is the opportunity to save a little bit of money when purchasing a home if you are going it alone. And even though the seller is technically paying your Realtor's fee, it is obviously being built into the sales price that the seller is going to require to get what is needed from the sale," Stan responded. "Every penny is important, and I appreciate your desire to be as frugal as possible. And even if you were buying a home in an area near where you lived and were intimate with that specific market, I still might not agree with you that going it alone is the best option. Other than a scenario where you are buying from someone you know, and you have inside knowledge of the property and situation, I would almost never advise going through this process without an experienced Realtor who has a superb track record.

"First and foremost, I believe it is critical that you have someone who can be an expert advisor and advocate for you throughout the home-buying process. While I will be that for you from a financing perspective, you need someone of equal capability to advise you through the purchasing phase. I'm going to ask you some questions to consider; you don't need to answer now. In this period of heightened regulation and compliance, do you know what to do with all the paperwork and what is needed when making a binding offer to buy? If you were to find your dream house, what do you do next? Are you a good negotiator in general, but specifically in real estate – and do you understand who you are negotiating with? What is the home you are buying really worth? I know you can investigate prices using multiple sources, but what is going on in the specific market where you wish to buy? And I don't just mean the city. I mean the specific pocket of that market. We probably have twenty-five different communities in and around our city that act as their own market and have different levels of desirability and price appreciation rates.

"You need someone who will be an educator to you, advising you on everything from general market conditions to specific property histories and neighborhood issues. Let's be honest, how well do you really know this area? I know there is plenty of information that you can gather from the Internet about prices and trends, but do you really know the kind of detail that you need to make the type of decision that merits the size of this investment? You have fallen in love with the area primarily based on your visits here for football games, but I'd encourage you that to make a wise decision, you need to rely on the assistance of someone who has a very clear understanding of how to get you the best value for your money.

"I also believe you will benefit greatly from working with someone who will take the time to listen to your needs and wants and will ask you detailed probing questions to determine what is most important to you. Once that information is obtained, your Realtor can do extensive homework on your behalf to help narrow your search into a manageable selection list. That will save you a tremendous amount of time, and it will make sure that the properties you actually take time to visit will fit your core list of things that are truly important. And you will be assisted with determining where compromise might be needed on your list of expectations versus what the market provides. Once you find a property worthy of buying, he or she can provide technical advice with making offers and engage with negotiations accordingly. Your Realtor will provide guidance regarding appropriate inspections and advice on handling any repair issues. He or she will walk you through every phase of the process right through the closing.

"In your specific situation, you will likely need to negotiate a price that will allow the seller to pay some or all of your closing costs. Remember that you have only $25,000 to work with. If you buy a home that requires most of this money to be used as your down payment, as was the case in the example we did at a $440,000 sales price, you would not have enough money left over to cover the costs related to buying in addition to paying your down payment. You would need to negotiate that into your contract so that you are asking for enough to cover what you need, but still properly pricing the home so that you are still getting the best price while building in this added component. Is that something you feel comfortable doing?"

He continued before either could answer, "I'd compare this similarly to working out or dieting. You know the basics – eat less and exercise and you will lose weight and get more fit. But what happens when you hire a trainer and a nutritionist to help you strategically start doing the right exercises and eating the right foods? Sure it will cost you a little more, but how much better are the results? In the end, do you not consider the extra money paid for additional help to be money well spent? Is a life better lived not worth a little extra in the long run? I hope you would agree that the answer to all of these questions is a resounding yes! I'd argue that whatever you think you are saving will ultimately result in a loss in some form or fashion. Yes, you can go it alone, and yes, you might save a little money on the price of the home. But for such a significant investment, does it not make sense to have someone help you make sure that you are truly making wise decisions that will wind up landing you not only the home of your dreams, but in the right area and at the right price?"

"Sold!" Dr. Santiago exclaimed. "You don't need to tell me anymore. This was all my idea anyway. Benita already mentioned to me several of the points you've made here so there is no need for us to even discuss it. We will get the application filled out for you tonight, and I'll touch base with you next week when I'm up your way doing a little house hunting. If you will forward me the name of a good Realtor who is a specialist in the area where we are looking, I would greatly appreciate it. I will touch base with you next week."

Stan smiled and said, "It was great spending time with the two of you today. I'll send you the name and contact information of a great Realtor and will keep an eye out for your application." With that Stan hung up the video conference, eased back in his chair, glanced over at me, and said, "Let's go get something to eat!"

What I learned from our visit with the Santiagos:

1. *Having a liquid emergency fund is by far the best way to handle a financial crisis.*
2. *The components of qualifying for a mortgage loan (income, credit, assets, and debt ratios) are the same for everyone.*
3. *A seller can help pay my closing costs if needed – but that must be negotiated.*
4. *I have to pay mortgage insurance unless I put 20% down.*
5. *On a conventional loan, the mortgage insurance can not only be paid several different ways, it can also go away after a time period.*
6. *Always use a qualified Realtor when buying and selling.*

10

CREATIVE REFINANCING

I went back over to Stan's office on Thursday afternoon to sit in on a meeting with a client who was retired and wanted to talk to Stan about buying a smaller house and figuring out if she should finance it. I got there about forty-five minutes early, and I'm glad I did. Stan told me that Josh had taken a call earlier in the day from a guy who was pretty perplexed and needed to talk to him. His name was Jerry Jackson, and Stan had promised to call him back before his afternoon appointment, so I got to listen in on the conversation.

When Jerry answered the phone, Stan said, "Jerry, this is Stan Smith over at My Home Mortgage. Our mutual friend Melissa Carlisle asked me to give you a call and said that you have some mortgage-related questions for me. Is now a good time to talk?"

Jerry, who Stan had on speaker phone, replied, "You bet, this is a great time to chat."

"Good deal," Stan responded. "I have a quick favor to ask you. You can probably tell that I have you on speaker. I have a young friend with me today who has been sitting in with me over the past couple of weeks just learning a little bit about what goes on in the mortgage world. Is it okay if he listens in on our conversation today?"

"That would be fine," Jerry responded. "As a matter of fact, he may even be able to provide some input to my dilemma, as part of it relates specifically to my daughter, who is a recent college graduate."

"Awesome," Stan said enthusiastically. "Then let's get started. Melissa did not give me any information about your situation, so tell me what's on your mind."

I immediately noticed the tone in Jerry's voice changed as he began to tell Stan his situation – it was almost apologetic. "Well, there is a longer story about how I got where I am right now, but I'll shorten it. The basic issue is that I'm short on cash. I've been able to pay my bills on time, so my credit should be good. I have two mortgages, one on the house that I live in and the other on a condo that I bought for my daughter when she went to college. We have decent equity on our home, thanks to putting a good bit down when we bought it and the appreciation from living there for twenty years. But with the turn in real estate, we owe about what the condo is worth on that mortgage. After graduation, my daughter relocated to another state. We couldn't sell the condo without losing money, so we decided to rent it. We are losing money on that from a monthly cash flow standpoint, but we are hoping that the market will continue to rebound and at some point we'll be able to sell it without taking a bath on it. My wife got pretty sick a couple of years ago, and we went through most of our cash reserves and then ran up two credit cards with pretty significant balances. She is better now, but she won't be able to go back to work for a while. We have made numerous modifications to our spending, and now we are able to pay everything from my income. But if we were to face any other hits to income or have a need for ready cash, we are going to be in a spot. So I'm just trying to figure out what to do."

Stan was very sincere with his response, and I could tell that he was really hurting for Jerry. "Jerry, I'm so happy for you that your wife is doing better. I think the thing that we learn more than anything else, when going through trials like yours, is that taking care of those we love is by far the most important thing we can do."

"I completely agree," Jerry affirmed, "but life does go on."

"That it does, my friend," Stan said as he was busy jotting down notes on his legal pad. "Let me ask you two questions. First, tell me a little about any other assets you may have, and second, would you mind if we take a quick look at your credit?"

"You can certainly check my credit," Jerry said. "As a matter of fact, I've actually been meaning to do that myself. But after talking to Melissa, I figured that would be something you would need to do if you were going to be able to help us, so just thought I'd let you do that. And we do have a good-sized 401K account with my employer. I've been with them for twenty-five years and have put money into the account every year until Barbara got sick a couple of years ago. I'm guessing the account is worth at least $250,000."

"Great!" Stan exclaimed. "I'm going to transfer you over to my assistant,

Josh. He will get a couple of pieces of information from you and have your credit in five minutes. When he has done that, he will transfer you back to me. He can get it done three times faster than I can." After getting Jerry's annual income figure and the address of the two properties, Stan transferred Jerry over to Josh.

While Jerry talked to Josh, I asked Stan what he was going to do. He was pulling something up on his computer while he answered me. "As opposed to explaining it to you, I'll let you and Jerry hear it at the same time. But it is very important for you to learn a couple of things here. First, things happen in life that aren't part of the plan. You've already seen a couple of really good examples of that in your time with me. Second, there are a lot of things that are a lot more important in life than money. If you will remember from our classroom discussion, how we handle our finances plays a role in every aspect of our lives. And last, know that the advice that I'm about to give Jerry is not the advice that I would like to give. Honestly, if he were in a different circumstance, I wouldn't. And by 'different circumstance,' I'm not talking about the difficult financial circumstance that he is currently in. He has actually done an admirable job staying on top of all that he has had to deal with over the past couple of years, and I'm betting his credit report will reflect that. If so, I have an idea of something that I think will help him."

Before I could ask another question, Josh walked in with the credit report, handed it to Stan, and asked if we were ready for him to transfer Jerry back to us. Stan said we were, and in less than five minutes from when Stan transferred Jerry over to Josh, he was back on Stan's line.

"Wow, that was fast," Jerry said as soon as Stan picked him back up. "I had no idea that you could run credit that fast."

"Yeah, modern technology has certainly helped quite a bit," Stan said with a chuckle. "Heck, when I started in this business, we had to order credit reports, and we had to wait two to three weeks before we got them. If you will excuse me for sixty seconds, I have another idea, but I need to get Josh's assistance with this."

As Stan walked out, I asked Jerry where his daughter had gone to school. He told me that he actually had two daughters, and both went to Ole Miss, which was their mother's alma mater.

Stan came back in and told Jerry, "Okay, we have about fifteen minutes before Mike and I have an appointment, so I'm going to be pretty straight to the point. I have a couple of suggestions that I want you to think about. You are welcome to give me your thoughts today, but I want you to discuss these with Barbara first and get back with me tomorrow to let me know her thoughts. And since this is all pretty top of mind, thoughts I'm coming up with as we talk, I may have other ideas to add to it later as well. I coach people to maintain a monthly budget that stays at or below 80% of their net income, have no personal debt other than mortgage debt, and it needs to ultimately be at 80% or less than the home's value. We'll come back to that in just a moment, but first I want you to know where my heart is and what I desire for my clients. I don't know what your other expenses are, but I'm guessing that based on what you have told me, those, plus the debts I see here on the credit report, are pretty much consuming everything you are currently bringing home each month."

"That's the problem," Jerry affirmed.

"I thought so," Stan said as he continued to instruct. "Do you know what the rate is on your two mortgages now?"

"Yes," Jerry replied. "We have had the loan on our home for eleven years. It is a refinance of the original loan. It is at 5.25%. The condo is a little better. We got it six years ago on an FHA loan at 4.75%. We co-signed that loan with our daughter, who was living there at the time."

"Okay," Stan said, "that helps. So here is my first thought. What I'm going to suggest might seem a little contradictory to what you might expect, and honestly it's a little out of the norm for my thoughts on getting out of debt in general. But it might be just the thing to get you in a better place, both now and long term. According to the credit report, you owe $116,000 on the mortgage on your primary residence, and the payment is $2,100. Does that include an escrow account for your taxes and insurance?"

"It does. We have escrow set up for both mortgages," Jerry answered. "Our insurance is $1,200 per year, and taxes are right at $3,000 per year."

"Perfect, that means your principal and interest are right at $1,750," Stan continued. "I also see that you have a $16,000 balance on your Visa and a $24,000 balance on your MasterCard. Those are both maxed out, as you explained earlier. They have required payments of $325 and $475, respectively. That all sound accurate?"

"It does," Jerry replied. "As I mentioned, we ran those credit cards up when we ran out of cash to pay for medical bills and other life stuff during Barbara's illness. I'm trying not to make excuses, but it is what it is."

"Again," Stan continued in a very genuine manner, "no one is beating you up here. I'm actually impressed at how you have handled the situation so responsibly. Our only goal here is to help."

Josh had come in while Jerry was speaking and handed Stan a piece of paper.

"Well, here is my first thought," Stan said in a very matter-of-fact way. "I think you need to refinance the current mortgage. It's not so much for a lower interest rate, although I do believe we could get you a rate that is lower than what you have now. I looked up your home's value online while you were talking to Josh, and it seems that the property should appraise for somewhere in the $305,000 range. Does that sound about right?"

Jerry responded, still in somewhat of a defeated tone, "Yeah, one of the discussions Barbara and I have had is whether or not we should just sell the home. But we love it here. And we wouldn't take less than $300,000, so that valuation seems pretty accurate."

"What I'd like to see you do," Stan continued, "is get some cash out of the property. You will need to get at least enough to pay off the credit cards and roll in the closing costs of the loan. This will allow you to immediately knock out both credit cards and reduce your monthly expenses by $800. That should be a huge relief to your monthly budget.

"I don't always like the idea of creating more mortgage debt to pay off non-mortgage debt, particularly credit card debt. From a financial standpoint, it makes sense to have the money borrowed at a lower rate and on a payment where the interest payment is tax deductible. But in general, I don't like the idea of paying off short-term debt with long-term debt. If I felt you were in a situation where you did not have a good commitment to avoiding car debt and credit card debt, I would probably not be advising you this way. But in your case, I'm confident that you manage those things well, and that your current situation has been created completely by an unforeseen life event and not from habitual over-spending. So for you guys, I think this is a great idea.

"I also would like to look at the possibility of taking enough cash from your primary residence, with this new refinance, to pay down the loan on the condo and potentially refinance it as well. If you plan to keep the condo for an extended period of time, we should look at this as well. According to the credit report, you owe $145,000 on it. I looked up the value on it, and it looks like it should be worth around $150,000. Since it is now an investment property, you'll probably want to borrow 75% of the value as that gives you the best pricing on an investment loan. Based on the payment on your credit report, the information I obtained on the taxes, and the assumed mortgage insurance payment, your principal and interest payment is right at $840 per month. I also assume that you pay a homeowner's association fee separately."

"You are pretty much dead on with all of your assessments," Jerry confirmed.

"Okay, If we were to do a 75% loan on it, that would be a loan amount of $122,500, so you'd need an additional $26,000 from the primary loan to cover the closing costs and principal payment on the condo if we refinance it. Tracking with me so far?"

"I'm with you," Jerry agreed.

"We'll come back to the payments in a moment, but first I want to make another suggestion," Stan said, this time with a little gleam in his eye. "Both new loans would need to be done on a conventional basis. By doing them that way and staying under 80% loan to value, you will be able to avoid mortgage insurance. Rates for conventional loans are tied to your credit score. As you surmised, you have paid your payments brilliantly. But having those two credit cards maxed out is hurting your score. Currently, your middle credit score is 695. While that is a good score, we would ideally like the score to be over 740. That is where you will get the best pricing.

He added, "I had Josh run an analysis on your scenario while we've been talking. Our credit reporting company has a model that we can use to perform 'what if' scenarios related to your credit score. I had him run a scenario to see what your score might improve to if you paid off the two credit cards. According to the results, your credit score would improve by 67 points if both of those cards were paid down to a zero balance. By doing that, your score would improve to 762. That would improve the rate that we would be able to offer you by at least .25% on both loans and probably by .375% on the condo loan. Does that make sense?"

"Sure," Jerry replied somewhat sarcastically. "But we don't have $40,000 lying around to do that. If we did, we wouldn't be in the dilemma we are in."

"I get that," Stan responded. "But I have another thought. We did a loan a couple of months ago for a co-worker of yours who also had money in his 401K account with your employer's administrator. He wasn't using the money for anything other than reserves on his loan, which is simply to show that there is cash available in an account above and beyond what is being used for the loan. But I remember reading through the terms of withdrawal, something we request for any retirement account that is being used as reserves, and noticing that there is an ability to borrow against the funds in the account. I'm certainly not suggesting that you pull the money out or even take out a long-term loan against your 401K account. However, you could take out a temporary loan and use it to pay off the credit cards. Since my recommendation is to pay them off anyway with the funds pulled out of the equity in the home, we would just pay back the 401K loan with the money from the mortgage. It would be more of a two-step process and would take a little longer, but it would tremendously help with the overall strategy on a long-term basis as it would help bring your mortgage rates down, thus giving you a lower payment. And paying the credit cards off would allow your score to improve enough to make that happen."

"That is a great idea!" Jerry exclaimed. "I had not even thought of that."

"If we do that," Stan kept going, "here is what the scenario would look like. We would add $75,000 to your current first mortgage. That should be enough to pay off the current balance and give enough extra to pay off the 401K loan, which will have been used to pay the credit cards off, plus enough to put the amount needed to get the other loan paid down to 75%, as well as roll in closing costs so you won't have to come out of pocket with any cash. If we do a thirty-year fixed-rate loan at 4.5%, the rate you'd be eligible for with the improved credit score, your principal and interest payment would be $968. If you decided to do a fifteen-year loan, the rate would be closer to 4%, and the payment would $1,413. Either way, it is a reduction in payment from what you are paying now, and it eliminates the current credit card payments. Even the fifteen-year loan would allow you to reduce your current overall monthly budget by over $1,000 per month. I like the idea of a fifteen-year loan only because of the lower rate. Remember that you can always prepay the principal on the loan at any point and for as much as you like with no penalty. So you could take the thirty-year loan now to get even more help with the monthly payment and just pay it off a lot faster if it makes sense to have the lower payment right now while you are getting things manageable again. Refinancing the condo would lower your principal and interest payment on that loan to $658 per month. That's assuming the $122,500 loan amount and a thirty-year fixed rate of 5%. That would reduce your overall monthly output by another estimated $250 by lowering your principal and interest as well as removing the mortgage insurance you are currently paying. This combination should be a huge improvement to your current situation and put you in a position to pretty easily get you back into a manageable budgeting situation.

"Let me also add that while I'm 100% confident that refinancing the mortgage on the primary residence is a good idea, refinancing the condo is a little more questionable. You are not really saving anything from a rate perspective in that situation. So while taking this extra step would certainly be an additional help, it is obviously not as significant as refinancing the primary mortgage. But if you plan on keeping the condo long term, I still like the idea of refinancing that loan as well. If you decide not to do that, we would just lower the loan amount slightly on the primary, since you wouldn't need the extra $26,000 to pay down the condo. That would lower the proposed payment a little more on the first mortgage, producing additional savings each month. It just wouldn't be quite as much as from an overall standpoint as refinancing the condo. So it's up to you and Barbara as to whether to do a refinance on both. But I definitely recommend this plan for the primary loan. And I suggest you check on that 401K loan as soon as you can. It may take a little time to get that in place and then a week or two to get the credit cards paid off and the credit score redone. That all make sense?"

"It certainly does," Jerry responded with confidence. "I will call my 401K administrator as soon as we hang up, and I'll review all of this with Barbara tonight. Can I call you tomorrow to run any questions by you that either Barbara or I may think of between now and then?"

"Absolutely," Stan responded. "As a matter of fact, I'm pretty sure I have a time slot tomorrow afternoon if you want to get on a conference call or even if you would prefer to come by the office and chat face-to-face. I'd love to talk a little more strategy with you. We really didn't get to talk much about other expenses, and I want you to have a plan of action to build back up your liquid savings as soon as possible. You know how important it is to have that emergency fund available. Another thing I want to talk to you about is setting up a home equity loan to have in place as a backup to your liquid emergency fund. If something happened and Barbara took a turn for the worse, you'd be better off borrowing on a home equity loan than a credit card. Sound good?"

"Sure does," Jerry replied, now sounding much more confident about his situation.

"Good deal, I'll talk to you tomorrow," Stan said as he hung up the phone and glanced over at me with a smirk as if to say, "That's how it's done!"

I had several questions that I wanted to ask Stan about this conversation, but they would have to wait. Wilma Johnson had just arrived for her meeting with Stan, and Emily was already escorting her back to Stan's office.

What I learned from the conversation with Jerry:

1. *Life happens; be prepared.*
2. *Nothing matters more than relationships with loved ones.*
3. *Sometimes even those who are prepared encounter difficulties.*
4. *Always pay my bills on time. It leaves more options available when I do.*
5. *If I have to have debt, mortgage debt is the best to have.*
6. *When I have plenty of equity in my home, get a home equity loan as an added measure of safety.*
7. *Fifteen-year loans are great, but only because they provide a better rate – not because they pay the debt faster. I can pay a loan off as fast as I choose regardless of term.*
8. *Sometimes it takes a little creativity to come up with the best solutions.*

11

DEBT FREE—NOW WHAT?

STAN'S final appointment of the day was with Wilma Johnson. Wilma was in her midsixties and had just lost Fred, her husband of forty-five years. Wilma, who had been a schoolteacher but hadn't worked in several years, and Fred, who was ten years older than Wilma, had retired a couple of years ago, and they were looking forward to traveling around this great country of ours and visiting many places that they had read about or had seen on TV. They had also talked about buying a little beach condo down in Destin where they could spend the winters and allow the rest of the family to use it for vacations during the summer. Fred's untimely heart attack put an end to all of those plans.

Now Wilma sat there in front of Stan, seemingly lost and confused about what to do next. She had decided to sell the home where she and Fred lived for the past thirty-plus years and buy something smaller. Maybe a condominium or a zero lot line home would be more manageable. She was hoping to find something in the neighborhood of their oldest child and his family to be a little nearer to her grandchildren. She had no idea what to do with the financing part of the deal. Fortunately for her, she had plenty of options, including paying cash if she chose to go that route. Should she sell her home before buying? Should she take out a mortgage or pay cash? If she needed a loan, what were the steps to take, and could she qualify? She had a multitude of questions on a heavy heart.

"Wilma," Stan began, "let me first tell you again how sorry I am that Fred is no longer with us. I actually had the opportunity to visit with him on a couple of occasions these past few years when he spoke to us at our Chamber meetings, and I got to know him pretty well many years ago when I helped the two of you with the loan that you have on your home now." Fred had been the dean of the business school at Lipscomb University for some twenty years after running his brokerage business for the first twenty-five years of his career and was well respected in the community. "He was a great man and meant a lot to our community."

"Thank you," Wilma replied. "It is amazing how we roll through life sometimes without stopping to notice the people that we impact. I know my Fred had a tremendous, positive effect, both in the business world and in the academic world. He was always too busy to stop and smell the roses. He just pressed forward every day to see who he could make a positive impact on. I do miss him."

"We all do," Stan agreed. "And I'm quite confident that with his economic sense he has left you in good shape financially."

"Oh, that is definitely true," Wilma concurred. "But that is also why I'm here. Fred always included me in financial matters and left me in great shape from that perspective. But he was also the one who was great with money and had the better sense of what to do in every situation. Now I need advice – maybe hoping for the same type of advice that Fred would give me in this situation. As much as I hate to leave our home, I just can't take care of it. And I certainly don't need anything that large anyway. I've found a couple of places that I'm interested in, but I'm not really sure how to go about making the transition. I'm equally concerned about how I should pay for the home I buy. Fred was a big believer in the benefit of having a mortgage, even when we could afford to pay off our loan. I've always been in favor of not having debt. I really don't like paying payments. But I do remember how you helped us when we refinanced our home a few years back, so I wanted to get your advice on what to do now."

"Well, I'm not going to tell you what to do," Stan said. "But I will help you make a good decision. The beautiful thing about your situation is that there are several good options. We just have to figure out one that is best for you."

"I really appreciate that," Wilma responded.

Stan said, "I want to ask you several questions, some that are financial in nature and some that are more personal that have more to do with your dreams and desires."

"That is fine," Wilma responded. "I am an open book."

Stan smiled as he looked directly at Wilma. "Tell me something. What does it mean to you to be debt free?"

Wilma answered, "Well, I suppose it means that you don't owe anyone anything. Isn't that what it's all about?"

"That is a great response and one that I would have expected you to give,"

Stan answered. "And while I can't necessarily argue that answer, I think I may have a better answer. For me, being debt free means that you have the ability to pay off debt anytime you want. In other words, you have enough cash on hand to write a check for whatever debt you may have. So any debt you have, you have by choice – not out of necessity. I hope this makes good sense to you. For example, if the only debt you have is a mortgage and you have more money in the bank than you owe on the mortgage, you are debt free. You simply choose to have a debt. While I realize that might not necessarily meet your definition of being debt free, I want to make sure you understand that concept. Many times, it makes good sense to have debt, particularly mortgage debt, even if you don't have to have it. I also understand your thought process and the desire not to feel obligated to pay anyone for money borrowed. So while I'm not suggesting at this stage that you use mortgage debt to purchase the home that you are considering, I just want to make sure that you understand that you can still be debt free even if you technically have a debt. As a matter of fact, there is a chance that I'll recommend that you pay cash for the home you are considering. I just want you to keep an open mind when considering all of your options."

"That is why I came to see you," Wilma replied. "And as you will see from my financial statement, I do have a debt, the mortgage on our home. And I also have plenty of cash so that I could pay it off if I chose to."

"Good deal. I have some more questions for you," Stan continued, "but before we get into those, let's take a look at the big picture and see where you are financially. I know Josh asked you to bring them with you, so let's take a look at the financial documents you brought me with the list of your assets and liabilities."

"Got it all right here, and I've put together a net worth statement detailing it for you," Wilma responded as she held up her folder of financial documents.

"Awesome," said Stan as he got out his pen and notepad as Wilma handed him a sheet of paper with all of her pertinent financial information.

Wilma Johnson Financial Overview:

Assets:	Value	Liabilities:	
House	$ 450,000.00	Mortgage:	$200,000.00
IRAs	$ 1,400,000.00		
Money Market:	$ 1,500,000.00		

Savings/checking:	$ 50,000.00		

Income:		Monthly expenses:	
Pension:	$ 2,300.00	Mortgage:	$ 2,000.00
Social Security:	$ 1,700.00	Necessities:	$ 1,500.00
		Entertainment:	$ 500.00

"As you can see," Wilma stated, "I've kept this pretty simple. It's just easier for me to process it this way. I will give you some details, though. The IRA money is in several accounts, but that is the total. The cash in the money market account is the life insurance money from Fred. Joseph, my financial planner, advised me to just park it there until we decide what to do about purchasing the home. I know I have too much money there right now, and I've probably got too much money sitting in my savings account. But it is safe there for the time being. As I mentioned, I only owe on one thing, and that is the mortgage. The payment listed counts the escrow account for taxes and insurance. The $1,500 I listed for necessities covers all of my monthly expenses. And that is probably a higher number than it really is most months. Same for my entertainment allotment – it is probably not that much either. But there are some trips that I want to take, so technically, it could wind up being more than that if you average it into a monthly expense. In essence, I just make sure that I don't spend more than my income from Fred's pension and my social security check."

"Well, I definitely see how living with Fred all these years has benefited you from a financial organization standpoint," Stan said. "You are amazing! And I know Joe very well. He is one of the best financial planners in town and will help steer you in the right direction with how to properly invest the money that you have. You mentioned taking some trips. I want you to tell me a little more about that. I also want to know your thoughts on buying that beach house that you and Fred always talked about. Last, I want to hear about your plans related to what and who you would like to give to charitably. I know you and Fred have always been very generous, so I assume that you have some thoughts on what you would like to do from that standpoint as well."

"Absolutely," Wilma replied. "You know that we have two children. We also have five grandchildren. And one of the things I did not list on that financial summary was that I also have a life insurance policy on me. Fred took out a whole life policy on me many years ago that is paid in full and has a death benefit of $500,000. I want all of that money to go to my children and grandchildren. But I also want to be generous to them while I'm still here. I want to have a little fun and get to see them enjoy some of it while I'm still around. And we have three or four organizations here in town that Fred always supported and I want to continue to support. They do great work, and it will be a huge honor for Fred if I can keep supporting them."

Wilma had more to say: I've always wanted to go to Europe, and one of the first places where Fred and I were going was the Holy Land. I just want to walk the same ground that Jesus walked when he was here on Earth. And I'm sure that it would be fun to go on a cruise, especially with my family. I've heard that there is no experience like a Disney cruise for the kids. That would be a lot of fun! As for the beach house, I'm not really sure about that. Our plan was to live down there during the cold months of the year and then let our kids and friends take advantage of it during the remainder of the year. I'm sure we would have gone there some throughout the year as well. But I just can't see myself staying down there all winter by myself. I guess I'll take your advice on that, and you can tell me what you think."

"Well," Stan said, "the beautiful thing is that you have within your means the ability to do everything you have described. How you go about accomplishing these things will be up to you, and you will have multiple options. Most of the planning I will leave for you and Joseph to figure out. Things like estate planning and protecting you from a tax perspective are right up his alley, and he will guide you brilliantly through that maze. You need a well-defined game plan on how to transfer your assets over to the ones you want receiving them in as tax efficient a manner as possible. Those types of decisions are way above my pay grade and certainly beyond my expertise, but I do think I can help you with some of the budgeting decisions. Take your current house for instance. I think I can help you with that. I also think I can help you with laying out a monthly budget that will help you accomplish most of what you were describing to me here. We need to get Joe involved as it relates to you starting to move some of your assets over to your children so that there won't be tax consequences for your estate. But again he is the expert on that; I'll leave that discussion for the two of you.

"Let's talk about your housing situation for a minute. I know the decision to move from the home you and Fred shared for so many years is a difficult one. But at this point, I gather that you have made the decision to make that move?"

"Yes," Wilma replied. "I have so many fond memories of experiences in that home. But at the end of the day, it is just too much for me to keep up with. And truly, it is just a house. The memories are in my mind and will never go away. I need something simple with no yard that I have to keep up with. Ideally I would love a little condo or some type of zero lot line home where I have a ground-level unit. I don't have any issue with stairs right now, but I can see that becoming a problem as my knees get older."

"I understand," Stan commented. "And I don't blame you. I've had a couple of knee surgeries myself, and I know there is going to be a day when I need a home with minimal steps. Let me change directions just a tad. How do you feel about having a monthly mortgage payment?"

Wilma replied, "Well, I've had one as long as I can remember. So I'm not really sure what it would be like not to have a house payment each month. I guess it would free up more money each month that I could do other things with, so that's probably not a bad idea."

"At this point have you looked at properties that have the characteristics you want in the area that you want to move?" Stan asked.

"I have," Wilma replied. "I haven't been out physically viewing properties, but I've looked at several online. Most of the homes I'm finding that fit the description of what I want, and are in the area that I want live, are in the $350,000 to $400,000 price range."

"Okay, here are my initial thoughts on financing the ultimate home purchase," Stan continued. "You have about $250,000 in equity in your current home. My first suggestion, which is pretty obvious, is that you need to put the money from the sale of your current home into the new home. Then you have one of two options as it relates to additional funds needed to purchase the new home. You can borrow the difference or take the money from your money market account and pay cash for the difference. And honestly, I could go either way on this. I love the idea of you having no payments at this point in your life. And you have certainly put yourself in a position that would allow this. But let's also look at what it would look like if you took out a loan to finance the difference. Depending on how much you borrow, you could likely do a fifteen-year loan, maybe even a ten-year loan, and have a payment that's less than what you're paying now. For example, you could buy a $400,000 home, put the $250,000 down on it from the equity of your current home, borrow the other $150,000 and have a payment on a ten-year fixed loan at $1,500 to $1,600 per month. Add taxes and the monthly HOA fee that you potentially have with a condominium, and you will still have a payment comparable to the one you have now.

"You are already used to paying a payment each month and have it sitting comfortably within your monthly budget. This would allow you to keep that extra money freed up and available for other investment opportunities or for charitable giving. If at any point in time the payment becomes difficult, you can always stroke a check and pay off the loan. The most cost-efficient time, as well as the easiest point in time that you will have to take out new financing, is at the time of initial purchase. So if having a payment comparable to the one you have now is comfortable, it might make sense to go ahead and keep your budget structured as you have it now. Does that make sense?"

Wilma replied as she nodded, "Yes, that makes perfect sense."

"Another thought I want to add while we are talking about real estate has to do with that beach home in Destin you have always dreamed about. I know you say that you have no desire to live there by yourself, and I understand that, even if only for a couple of months out of the year. But here's a thought: What if you bought a place in Destin as an investment property? This is another idea that we will want to run past Joe, but I think this could accomplish several things for you. Assuming you are truly buying it as a rental property, and one that could rent for weeks at a time, maybe even months at a time, it would provide an additional source of revenue for you every month. This would be a great way to diversify some of the money that is currently in the money market account that you will likely want to invest in something earning a little better return than what the money market pays. This will really help diversify your investment portfolio as most of the rest of your investments are tied up in the market in some form or fashion. And since you own the property, you can establish the rent schedule. You can decide when you want to go and spend time there yourself and for how long. You can also schedule weeks for your family to have use of the property, allowing it to be rented the remainder of the time.

"If that is something you are interested in, and Joe agrees that it's a good idea, I'll introduce you to Kim Keys, a friend of mine in Destin, who is a phenomenal real estate agent. I met her seven or eight years ago when my wife and I bought a vacation home there. She can help you find the exact property that fits all of your requirements, and she can also connect you with a good property management company that can manage all of the rental clients for you. You obviously give up a little bit of your monthly income by paying a property manager to handle the property for you, but it is well worth it to avoid the hassle of managing it yourself."

Wilma's eyes lit up at hearing this. I could tell that his thought had never really crossed her mind. "Stan," she exclaimed, "I think that may be the best idea I've heard in a long time! Fred and I spent many wonderful vacations in Destin, and it had been a dream of ours to own a home there. I also developed some friendships down there as well as having friends here who own homes there. Doing what you suggest would allow me to have a place there without feeling that I had to live there for any length of time on my own, but still get to go there when I want. I would love to host both of my children's families there for as many weeks out of the year as they want to come."

"Well, it's definitely something we will run by Old Joe, but I think he will like the idea of the diversification to go along with the monthly income it will provide," Stan told her. "And the fluctuations in the income, due to taking seasonal renters versus nonpeak renters into consideration, won't be an issue as you are not relying on that income for your monthly budget. Depending on the price you pay and Joe's recommendation on how to invest the money from the money market will depend on my recommendation for financing that type of property. Interest rates are not as good on investment properties as they are on a primary residence. So if this is something you think you might want to do, you'll need to get a good idea of the price range. It might make sense to borrow a little more on the home you buy that you're going to live in versus borrowing it against the home in Destin.

"For example, let's say Joe wants you to invest $400,000 to $500,000 of the money market fund into real estate. You could buy a $600,000 home in Destin and pay cash for it while borrowing up to $320,000 on a $400,000 primary residence that you purchased here in Nashville. You don't want to borrow more than 80% of the value of the home you buy here. But if you buy a $600,000 home there and a $400,000 home here, the total is $1 million. You have $250,000 coming from the equity in your current home and the $400,000 to $500,000 to move from your money market into real estate. So you would need to finance between $250,000 and $350,000. Now if you do that, we may want to consider a thirty-year loan on the home here to keep your payment in a more manageable level for your budget. If you borrowed $320,000 here, your payment would be around $1,700 per month. If you add $500 to cover taxes and the HOA fee, you are at $2,200 per month. That is a little more than you are paying now. But a home in Destin that is that nice might bring you as much as $2,500 per month net. So you could in effect pay your mortgage here with the rental income from the property there. Obviously, this strategy does carry some risk with it as the rental income is not guaranteed. But because of your incredible asset strength, the risk is minimal. And if you are keeping the total payment in line with what you are paying now, your risk is minimized. We can talk to my friend Kim in Destin and get more specific numbers related to costs of properties and expected rental figures. And at the end of the day, you will still have plenty of cash to pay the loan balance off if the monthly payment becomes a deterrent for you.

"Because of your age, there is going to come a time pretty soon when you will start being required to draw the IRA out on an annual or a monthly basis as well due to tax laws. As long as we keep your budget within the framework of the income coming from the pension, the social security, and the rental income from your vacation home, you can design a plan that will allow you to give all of that extra income away. It can go to family or any charitable organization you wish to support. Again, this is something that Joe will help you with. I just wanted you to be thinking about it ahead of time. The thing I love more than anything else about what you're doing is you are putting a roadmap in place before you make any decisions. You would be shocked at how few people actually sit down and plan out the way they will spend their money and have a plan for giving their money during retirement or as retirement approaches."

"Stan," Wilma said, "I can't thank you enough for your time today. I am very grateful that Fred had such good friends like you that I can lean on to give me great advice."

"You are certainly welcome," Stan replied. "I will give Joe a call and let him know what we have discussed. I suggest your next step be to set up a meeting with him to review the information we have gone over today. I will also email Kim and copy you, introducing the two of you, and ask her advice on homes in Destin and give her a little insight on what you are trying to do. You can discuss with her the specifics of the homes you would like to look at."

With that, Wilma hugged Stan's neck and left. Stan walked out of his office to talk to Josh. I was still taking notes.

What I learned from our meeting with Mrs. Johnson:

1. *Being debt free doesn't necessarily mean that I have no debt – a better definition of being debt free is that I have enough savings to pay off the debt if I choose.*
2. *If I have debt, mortgage debt is the best type to have.*
3. *Owning real estate can provide significant advantages in helping me diversify my investments one day.*
4. *Financing my primary residence offers better terms than investment properties.*
5. *Be organized – it will be so much easier to make sound financial decisions when everything is detailed and accounted for accurately.*
6. *Think outside the box to maximize results.*
7. *Having a financial advisor to guide me from an overall perspective will be a must.*

12

THE END OF THE BEGINNING

AFTER our meeting with Mrs. Johnson, Stan asked if he could buy me lunch the next day. He wanted to go over what I'd learned the past couple of weeks. We agreed that we'd meet at his office and go from there. I spent most of the night compiling a pretty good list of things I'd learned and was looking forward to sharing them with Stan. And when I say "most of the night," I literally did not sleep that night. It was a great exercise for me and really wasn't anything new for me to pull an all-nighter. I was also about to ask Stan a pretty significant question, too, so I was understandably a little nervous. I had made some monumental changes in my thought process, and many of my thoughts on finances had taken a 180 degree turn. Although it was still very early in the action phase, I was rocking the planning phase. How fast I could get out of the mess I was in would depend to a large degree on how much money I could make over the next several months to go along with several other modifications being made to my monthly budget. But one thing was for sure, the mess was not going to get any worse. I had learned a lot more than I expected in a short time and actually surprised myself at the amount of notes I'd taken.

When I got to his office on Friday, it was clear that I'd missed the memo about this being a casual Friday. Everyone was wearing jeans and either sweaters or sweatshirts, looking much more comfortable than I felt in my shirt and tie. Emily led me back to Stan's office where I sat and listened to him finish up a conversation. Not to my surprise, he had on a gaudy orange sweatshirt with a huge VOLS stitched on his chest. I couldn't tell who he was talking to, but I knew it wasn't a client. He was discussing a specific guideline related to gift funds and wrapped up the conversation talking trash to whoever it was about how badly the Wildcats were playing. When he hung up, I asked him if every conversation he had revolved around some sporting event. He responded with a grin, "Family, sports, Bible, and mortgage, that's pretty much all I know enough about to carry on a decent conversation!"

I laughed and told him again how much I appreciated the opportunity he'd given me over the past few weeks to follow him around.

"I'm anxious to hear what you have learned," Stan replied. "We have been very fortunate that our various meetings have produced a wide variety of situations and life stages. We've covered a pretty diverse group."

"Yeah, that has probably been my favorite part of the time I've spent with you," I told Stan as I handed him a piece of paper. "I reviewed my notes from the past couple of weeks and jotted down a list of the most important concepts I've learned. Well, I guess I wasn't just learning all of them, but I was certainly given a great reminder of the ones that I already knew. There were more than twenty, but I wanted to keep the number to a manageable group, so I kept it at twenty. I'm not really sure what to call the list. But I'm pretty confident that if I follow the instruction of each one, I'm going to be financially successful. And I'm guessing that the financial success will carry over into other areas of my life as well. I think the overriding lesson that I learned is how much personal finances play a role in people's lives. It is one thing to experience it in my life, but that fact truly became real as I saw it played out in the lives of everyone we met with." I paused for a moment as I watched him review the list I'd prepared.

TOP 20 THINGS I'VE LEARNED FROM STAN

1. You must have a plan for your money. Failing to plan is planning to fail.
2. While spending is fun, saving is the key to long-term financial success.
3. Avoid impulse buying – particularly with-big ticket purchases.
4. Compound interest is a saver's best friend.
5. Budgeting may be boring, but it is the difference maker.
6. Live within 80% of the net income you bring home each month – bare minimum.
7. Give away at least the first 10% and save at least the second 10%.
8. Discipline is critical – in life and in finance.
9. Borrow money only for your primary residence and for income-earning assets.
10. Pay off your credit cards at the end of every month.

11. Your credit score is very important – *always* pay your bills on time.

12. Having no credit, thus no credit score, is not as good as having good credit with no debt.

13. If at any point it is absolutely necessary to borrow to make a purchase that is not a home or an income-producing asset, have a plan to pay the loan off quickly.

14. Buying a home is more financially rewarding than renting.

15. When you borrow to buy a house, either put 20% down or have an action plan to get to that equity position as soon as possible.

16. Once you get to 80% loan to value, it likely makes more sense to invest versus paying down the mortgage. Banks use arbitrage to make money. I can do the same.

17. Cash is king. Even if you have mortgage debt, having enough money to pay off your mortgage is normally a better position to be in than no mortgage and no money.

18. If you are married, all financial decisions are made together as a team.

19. Having people on your team is a must. Everyone needs an awesome financial planner, and it will almost always make sense to hire a Realtor when buying and selling a home.

20. Take a positive role in the lives of others, helping them when I can, and connecting them with others when that is more prudent.

After giving him an opportunity to review my list, I asked him, "So, what do you think?"

He looked up at me and gushed, "I think this is awesome! It is quite a list. Heck, you could write a whole book on the points you have made here and create a small chapter for each of these topics."

"Well, I'm not much of a writer," I responded. "I've always thought of myself as a numbers guy. But after what I've learned this past month, I wouldn't even consider myself a really good numbers guy. At least not up until this point. I definitely agree with you, though, it is a pretty comprehensive list. Instead of writing a book, I have a better idea. I've given it a lot of thought, and I'd like to start teaching these concepts to my own clients." Stan looked at me somewhat inquisitively but never said a word. I continued, "Hey, I'm good with numbers. Maybe I've been misguided somewhat with my own actions from a financial perspective, but I think that only gives me a better platform from which to preach the message. I want to improve my own situation first, but then I want to teach these lessons to others."

I was hoping Stan would get the message that I was trying to hint at, but it wasn't sinking in. After staring at me for what seemed like an eternity, he asked, "How do you plan to do that?" I grabbed his forearm with my hand and looked straight into his eyes and exclaimed, "I want you to hire me! I want to work for you. I want to teach people the lessons that I've learned from you the past month. I would love to say that I'd work for free, but you have seen my financial situation. So you know I can't do that. But I'll work for as little as possible. I've already reconstructed my budget, and I'm making some other radical changes to my lifestyle and spending habits. I just want to learn more from you and be able to teach it to others."

I could tell that Stan was a little caught off guard with what I asked him. He had been staring directly at me, looking me right in the eye, while I was talking. The moment I finished, his eyes drifted away, and he stared out the window. It was probably only ten to fifteen seconds, but it seemed a lot longer than that.

When he turned back to me, I saw that same gleam in his eye that I'd seen now at least half a dozen times over the past month. He simply said, "I think we might be able to figure a way to make that work. I'd like to see you knock some of your debt out first, and I'll need a little time to put a plan together for you that will help you learn the business while assisting me. But I think we can figure something out. Let's go get some lunch, and we can talk some more."